Mental Models

A Step by Step Guide to Improving your Critical Thinking, Decision Making and Problem Solving through Effective Mental Modeling

By Adrian Kirk

engaging in the rendering of legal, financial, medical or professional advice. The content within this book has been derived from various sources. Please consult a licensed professional before attempting any techniques outlined in this book.

By reading this document, the reader agrees that under no circumstances is the author responsible for any losses, direct or indirect, which are incurred as a result of the use of information contained within this document, including, but not limited to, — errors, omissions, or inaccuracies.

Table of Contents

Introduction

This book contains vital information on how to properly and effectively use various mental models in improving your quality of thoughts, attitudes, and behaviors. Mental models lay the foundation on how you view and understand the reality of the world. Beyond your thoughts, these are also reflected on how you treat other people around you. As such, having the right mental models could elevate you as a highly capable and well-respected individual.

In the most basic terms, mental modelling refers to the principle of simplifying complex information in order to transform said information into manageable and actionable points. If you could excel at this, you would be able to react better and faster without sacrificing the quality of your thoughts and decisions.

However, when taken to the extreme, useful mental models could turn into potentially harmful schemas, such as stereotypes, prejudice, and various forms of cognitive biases.

Fortunately, even if you are currently saddled with less than optimal mental models, you may still improve them through your solid commitment and regular practice. You can learn how to do this, and more by absorbing

and reflecting upon the contents of this book.

Thanks for downloading this book. I hope you

enjoy it!

Chapter 1–Understand Your Schemas

Schemas are organizational concepts that a person can use to create mental structures that would simplify how he or she thinks and perceives others and their surroundings. When used in proper and appropriate ways, they can be helpful since humans are constantly bombarded with large amounts of information everyday. Using schemas to interpret these pieces of information quicken the thinking process and allow one to arrive at conclusion or decision without giving out much effort.

For example, a young boy forms his schema for a horse by being taught that it is a large animal covered with fine hair, has four legs, and a tail. Using this schema, he might call similar looking animals such as a cow when he first sees it. After all, the cow fits the schema he has learned about a horse: a hairy, large, four-legged animal with a tail. If his parents were to correct his schema by pointing out the differences between the horse and the cow, the young boy would be able to modify the current schema he has about the horse and gain a new schema for a new and entirely different animal.

What if the boy somehow encounters a miniature horse? If he already has a schema for a dog, he might identify this particular animal as a dog. Again, his parents have to explain to him that the miniature horse differs actually from a dog and is actually related to the type of horse he knows. It would then give the boy a chance to further refine his schema of a horse. Through his observations and the teachings of his parents, he now knows that horses can either be large or small animals, provided that said animals possess the other defining characteristics of a horse, such as the shape of the face, appearance of the mane, length of the tail, among others.

It should be noted that overdependence on schemas have drawbacks as well. Because of its nature, a schema can lead you to focus only on the characteristics and information that are already aligned with your current beliefs and ideas about someone or something. This would then cause more complicated mental and social issues over time, like when a person develops stereotypes or forms any of the different types of cognitive biases.

A Brief Historical Background on Schemas

Frederic Bartlett, a British psychologist, first used the concept of schemas as one of the key components of his learning theory. He proposed that a person's understanding and interpretation of the world is founded upon a vast network of abstract ideas or mental structures. He did not, however, use the term "schema" in his work, but his theory bears hallmarks of the early researches conducted in this particular area of interest in the field of developmental psychology.

It was actually Jean Piaget who first introduced and popularized the term "schema" through his many works on childhood development. To be specific, Piaget explains in one of his theories that schemas are not merely categories of knowledge. Instead, for him, a schema is also the process of gaining knowledge that turns into one's mental structures. By following his line of thinking, you could say that schemas are moving in a cyclic loop. A person constantly adapts to his or her surroundings, taking in new information and learning new concepts or skills. Over time, and with more experience, the existing schemas are replaced or changed by new schemas that better reflect that person's environment.

Types of Schemas

Although Piaget's works are more focused on childhood development, his explanations on schema have led researchers to discover the different types of schema. Across cultures and beyond boundaries, here are the most common types of schemas possessed by people:

Person Schema

Scope: Knowledge about specific individuals that a person may or may not know personally but has interacted with at some point in his or her life.

Examples

a. You believe that all priests speak in a calm and composed manner. However, upon attending the mass headed by the newly assigned priest at your local parish, you discovered that priests can also sound passionate and, at times, fiery while giving out their sermon. Though the priest remains an advocate of peace and love, he also has strong opinions on morality and how society can change for the better.

b. Popular comedian Robin Williams is assumed by many to be a prototype of an extraverted individual due to the loud and fun personality of the characters he typically portrays on movies and TV shows.

Social Schema

Scope: One's general knowledge about the expectations or demands of society on how a person should behave in a particular social situation.

Examples

a. While attending a basketball game for the first time, you noticed that many fans yell or cheer whenever the team you are rooting for scores. This happens frequently enough for you to make an association between yelling and cheering during sporting events. Soon, you find yourself yelling and cheering in support for the team, too. At this point, you have finally adapted said social schema as your own.

b. Your classmate, Charles, tends to be reserved and stoic while in the classroom. Because of this, you expected him to behave similarly during a class party. Much to your surprise, Charles acted differently during the recent get-together of the class. He seemed to be more outgoing and carefree than his usual self. As a result, you are beginning to see him in a new light, though you are not quite sure yet if the change in his behavior was natural or if it had been brought out by the alcohol that he had consumed during the party.

Self Schema

Scope: A person's knowledge about his or her current self, ideal self, and/or future self.

Examples

a. Back when you were in high school, you have learned the distinctive traits of what makes a person either a geek or a jock. Upon assessing your own interests and behavior, you found out that you are one of the jocks. Even if you were also keen about video games and browsing through the Internet for cool stuff to do, your athletic pursuits seem to overpower the rest of your interests. You also enjoyed physical education class and hanging out with the other kids from the basketball club. As such, you began identifying yourself more with this group, mimicking some of your peers' behaviors, and taking their point of view when it came to issues about your life as a high school student.

b. Kyle has a self-schema about a healthy and a sickly person. Because of this, he actively strives to become a health-conscious individual. Most of his day-to-day decisions are centered on what would keep him fit and illness-free. From what he would eat for each meal to how frequently he should go to the gym in a week, Kyle makes it a point to always choose food and activities that can help him maintain his health and physique. He even tries to avoid going out with friends if they wish to spend the evening at a bar to avoid second-hand smoke, and to prevent himself from giving in to the temptation of consuming alcohol.

Event Schema

Scope: Patterns of behaviors exhibited by a person in conjunction with what he or she believes about what one should do and say during a certain event

Examples

a. You are planning to attend the birthday party of your niece with your son. Since he has not yet been to any birthday party before, he asks you if the party is the same as having a playdate with the other kids. You explain to him that birthday parties are different because there will be cake, singing, and gifts. Even though the invitation does not state these activities in particular, you have a social schema for birthdays from the past parties you have attended yourself. This social schema serves as the reference point for you to give others information that they do not have themselves.

b. Based on your experiences, you know by heart the sequence of behaviors that happen whenever you dine at a family restaurant. First, you and your companions enter the restaurant of your choice and wait to be ushered into a table by the receptionist. Then, you would order for drinks from the waiter, while perusing the menu. Once everyone has made their choice, the waiter would come back to your table and take everyone's orders. Food and beverages are usually served within the lead time specified by the waiter. After consuming the meal, the bill must be paid before leaving the restaurant.

Roles of Schemas in Your Daily Life

Schemas, regardless of their accuracy, completeness, and level of detail, are ever-present among humans from all walks of life. It is not only a tool that young children use to get a better understanding of the world.

Adults frequently rely on schemas as well in the following different aspects of their lives, sometimes without even realizing that they are doing so.

Acting like filters, schemas can either enhance or subdue the qualities of a person, object, or situation. This makes it easier for people to classify information, like when an employer pigeon-holes a job applicant for his educational background.

Schemas can help one predict what will happen next after a particular event has transpired. For example, if a student fails to submit his assignment on time, he is likely expecting to receive at the end of the class a note about his recent poor performance from his teacher to his parents.

Many people use schemas to enhance their level of information retention and recall. Color-coding your possessions and your roommate's, for example, makes it easier for both of you to remember which towel belongs to whom.

Schemas are useful for filling in the gaps when the knowledge you have about a certain event or issue is limited. For instance, a news report about a woman missing for several days does not specify whether the investigators have found evidence about whether or not the missing woman is still alive. Based on your current knowledge about cases like this, you might automatically assume that the woman is likely dead at this point.

A type of schema called the "multiple necessary cause schema" allows a person to come up with two or more probable causes for a particular outcome or event. These probable causes have varying degrees of likelihood, depending on the context of the situation, and may usually be confirmed when one of these schemas has been determined as the correct cause.

Because schemas are typically shared among those who belong in the same culture, using these mental structures serves as foundations for communication shortcuts. This means that most words could have an attached schema to them based on their respective cultural connotations. Schemas are formed based on one's life experiences. Unfortunately, even when faced with opposition and contradictory information, established mental models can be quite difficult to change or entirely remove.

Therefore, the human mind is hard-wired to create its own version of reality and how things work, and even if this said version becomes inaccurate or unhelpful, people are inclined to keep on using them. That is why one's experiences during the earlier phases of human development are critical of how that person would turn out later on. The schemas that have been formed during these stages are carried on to adulthood, impacting not only one's perception of the world but of himself or herself as well.

Examining Yourself for Poor Schemas and Weak Mental Models

As mentioned earlier, people have a tendency to hold on to old beliefs. The effect of doing so influences your attitudes and behaviors, even without your prompt. The way to ensure that your schemas still serve you well be to examine yourself for mental models that need to be improved upon. After all, awareness and recognition are the first steps of almost every effective self-improvement program there are.

To guide you on this, here is an activity that would help you identify the schemas that are governing your thought processes. Follow these steps and carry them out before proceeding to the next chapters.

Step #1: Get yourself a notebook or journal.

This would serve as your personal log of your progress in your endeavor to improve your mental models. As you continue reading this book, keep that notebook or journal on hand so that you can refer to them when you have to reflect on how the concepts that would be discussed in later chapters apply to your personal experiences and goals in self-improvement.

Step #2: Think about your beliefs that you have had for as long as you can remember.

Regardless of whether you have come up with these beliefs on your own or you have just adapted from somebody else, list them down in a concise but sufficiently descriptive terms. To make your list more comprehensive, think of at least five believes you have that would fall under each main type of schema:

a.   Personal Schemas

b.   Social Schemas

c.   Self Schemas

d.   Event Schemas

Step #3: Reflect on the beliefs you have listed down for each category of schemas.

Without learning yet the makings of a weak mental model, analyze your personal views about the beliefs you are holding on to. As a guide, ask yourself these questions during your self-reflection:

- "Is this belief still accurate?"

- "Am I being limited in any way by this belief?"

- "Does this belief strengthen me as a person or not?"

For example, you believe that eating fast food products is a way of treating yourself well since doing so allows you to enjoy your favorite comfort food without the hassle of cooking it yourself. Ask yourself if this is actually a valid self-care method. Do you feel good about yourself after eating fast food items? Does it contribute anything else to your life?

Write down your reflections on your journal so

that you will not have to come up with them again later on. After you have gone through the succeeding chapters of this book, check back on your responses on these questions and see anything has changed on how you view your beliefs.

At this point, you are not likely aware of how to effectively change some of your long-held beliefs for the better. That is perfectly alright since you still have a long way to go. Just keep in mind that you do not have to see the world as you have always done. Change can be good when you have good intentions, and it is managed properly. Furthermore, what is true in the past does not mean that it will always be true. Similarly, even if you have learned how to do things in a certain does not mean that you have already learned how to do it best. Your current schemas might be dictating how you think and act right now, but you can regain control over them once you have fully understood how to build and maintain stronger mental structures.

Chapter 2 – Challenge Your Existing Models

Changing one's schemas for the better is an achievable feat if you have an open mind for learning new things. There are various ways to go about this, but most experts agree that two primary processes govern one's adaptability: assimilation and accommodation.

Assimilation

As initially proposed by Jean Piaget, assimilation is the process of taking in new information and incorporating them into an individual's current knowledge and ideas. Due to its nature, it is considered highly subjective. The same piece of information is assimilated differently by two persons because each can only modify their respective personal experiences and current beliefs.

Assimilation is one of the core techniques used to learn about the workings of the world. Experts have noted that young children assimilate new information naturally, consequently building up their confidence in further exploring their environments and interacting with those around them.

More research shows that assimilation does not only occur during childhood. Adults take in and process information based on their experiences. They would then interpret these new ideas and incorporate them into the existing structures in their minds. Depending on the scope and intensity of the experience, this could entail small or large adjustments to the thought processes of the said person.

How Assimilation Works

According to the theories on learning presented by Piaget, assimilation is the easiest method that one could employ to acquire knowledge and improve one's existing schemas. This is mainly because the foundation is already laid out within a person's mind. The real effort begins when one has to figure out how new information fits in with his or her current mindset and beliefs.

Take, for example, the children who subconsciously apply the principles of assimilation without even knowing it. They are always trying to make sense of their environment and the surrounding people. By comparing and contrasting their experiences versus what they know at a given point, they are able to perceive reality according to what they have been taught or what they have learned on their own previously. This also means that a child's understanding of the world heavily influences how they interpret new information and experiences, filtering out, at times, the pieces that do seem to fit especially when there is no one else to guide them through this process.

To further illustrate this concept at work, there are more examples of scenarios wherein the person performs assimilation:

- An elementary student trying to learn how to play a new piano piece

- A mother figuring out how to use the new microwave oven by reading through the manual and trying out different settings

- A young boy who, upon seeing a model of a car out that he has never seen before, points to the vehicle and yells "Car!"

- A newly hired sous chef undergoing an orientation about the executive chef's rules in the kitchen

Take note of how new information is being processed by the individuals presented in the examples given above. Each person is just adding on to their existing knowledge and beliefs. If, however, the new experience or information causes significant or complete changes in a person's mindset, then the learning process at play is no longer assimilation, but rather, accommodation.

Accommodation

If you are altering your existing schemas because of a newly acquired information or experience, then your mind is engaging with the process called accommodation. First proposed by Jean Piaget as part of the adaptation process, many experts in human development suggests that this is a life-long activity that is necessary in order to maintain and develop relationships with others, and to remain functional in the ever-changing world.

Piaget first noted this phenomenon while observing his children learn the different types of animals. As he had explained, his daughter had an existing schema for a dog which is its four legs. Therefore, she automatically believed that any animal with four legs is also a dog. When taught about cats, which also have four legs, she finally learned that not every four-legged animal is called a dog. She had undergone the process of accommodation, thereby revising her current schema for dogs and adapting a schema for cats.

Following this instance, Piaget suggests that accommodation does not only mean changes into one's existing schemas. The process can also lead to the creation of new schemas that would better define other schemas related to it. As more information is acquired and accommodated by a person, the more refined and nuanced a schema becomes. As a result, the said person would have more detailed ideas and beliefs about other people and the world in general.

How Accommodation Works

Accommodation does not only occur during one's childhood. Many experts agree that this actually takes place throughout a person's entire lifetime. As one gains a new experience, he or she has to accommodate the new information that has been brought about by the said experience in order to ensure that one's thoughts or beliefs are always in accordance with the reality of the world.

For example, Andrea has been raised by parents that taught her a schema against a certain group of people. Because of the beliefs and manners that he has adapted from his family, she develops a prejudice against the said social group.

Upon entering the university, however, Andrea is faced with a community that accepts all groups of people, including the one that she is prejudiced against. Being far away from home, she has no choice but to interact with people who have different beliefs about her towards that group of people. At a certain point, she has also directly interacted with a member of that group.

Over time and continued exposure, Andrea finally realizes the error in her upbringing and current beliefs. This significant change in her mindset and regard towards the said group of people happens as a result of her accommodation of the schemas presented and exhibited by those around her. Compared to assimilation, wherein she would have accepted the fact that some people do not have ill thoughts about that social group, accommodation has caused a more dramatic change in her beliefs and future behavior. Assimilation and accommodation do not work exclusively from one another. Neither process is inherently better than the other in all situations. Instead, each process complements the other, thereby making both of them essential for the healthy development of one's cognitive skills.

This has been noted by Piaget during one of his earlier case studies on the sensorimotor stage of development among infants. Babies interact with their environments, giving them sensory and motor experiences at the same time. Though there is no exact rule governing which process would be adapted by the babies to interpret this information, some of their experiences would be assimilated, while some information could become accommodated.

Again, this is not limited to the early stages of development. Everyone goes through these processes to continually gain knowledge and improve upon their current mindsets.

Recent studies on human development recommend the establishment of a healthy balance between assimilation and accommodation. By doing so, a person would gain a sense of stability wherein he or she can adapt to changes quickly and more effectively.

Furthermore, even though the imitation of other's schemas could help reform one's negative schemas, a strong sense of self is still necessary in order to prevent being vulnerable towards all kinds of external influences. This means that it is perfectly alright to learn by imitation of the words and actions of those around you. However, you should still listen to your own intuition and understanding of the world in determining whether your attempt to change would turn you into a better version of yourself.

Assimilation or Accommodation?

What factors determine the way new information would be processed? A group of researchers have noted that it is not possible for the same information to be assimilated and accommodated at the same time. These processes work in opposition to the other, so a person has to personally make the choice between the two.

What tips the scale in favor to one side over the other? This step of the process usually happens without much conscious thought on which of the two routes would be taken by the person. Still, there are people who carefully introspect about these matters. Upon analyzing their accounts, researchers believe that the following qualities and context affect the person's decision:

Assimilation

People who engage with assimilation aim to maintain the status quo. They are keen on keeping their current schemas intact. New information is treated as an addition to their knowledge, not as a replacement. Think of it as a person who enjoys collecting books. He enjoys buying a new book and finding a place for it somewhere on his shelves.

Accommodation

People who welcome total or partial alterations to their existing schemas about a particular topic are practicing the principles of accommodation. Going back to the example given above, this is more similar to a scenario wherein the person who bought a new book finds out that there simply is no more space left for the recent addition. Because of this, he decides to buy a new bookshelf that is large enough to serve as storage for this new book as well the other books that he might buy in the future.

In any given situation, a person would have to choose between assimilation or accommodation. This is dependent on the person's tendencies, level of open-mindedness, and what new information has been learned. Figuring out where you fall in the spectrum could prove to be helpful for you in successfully removing negative schemas and/or improving your weak schemas.

Challenging Your Current Models through Assimilation and Accommodation

To illustrate the probability of changing your current schemas through either assimilation or accommodation, picture this scenario and take note of how you would react upon witnessing it.

Your neighbor has a son named Matt. This boy is known to be sweet and respectful towards everyone. One day, as you were drawing your window curtains open, you catch him throwing a snowball at the windshield of your car. This does not fit with what you know about Matt's personality. You have never expected such a rude behavior from this boy.

Before reading on, take a pause and examine closer your initial reaction. How do you interpret Matt's action? Is he doing this on his own, or is he being influenced by another person? Is it really out of character for him to do so, or is this a side of him that you just did not know before this incident?

Run through the scenario inside your head and internalize your thought processes and feelings about being in this kind of situation. Once you are ready, compare your reactions with the following explanations, and find out which principle you have applied to challenge your current schema about Matt's personality.

<u>Assimilation</u>

You are assimilating this new information about Matt when you dismiss the behavior he exhibited as an influence of another person on him. Without further proof, you believe that he most likely did not intend any harm by throwing a snowball at your car. He might have just witnessed a classmate doing this behavior before and decided to copy it in order to experience it for himself.

In this case, you have not completely revised your schema about Matt's personality. You have simply added new information to your current knowledge about this kind and polite boy. Other than his positive traits that he normally displays, Matt apparently has a mischievous side to him. You might also suppose that he is easily influenced by his peers or his current environment.

Accommodation

When this incident has caused to you to reevaluate your opinion about Matt, then you are accommodating this new information about his behavior, and using as a basis to change partially or completely the way you regard this boy.

Challenging your current schemas through assimilation and accommodation requires you to be open about learning new things and accepting new beliefs about others and the world in general. Fortunately, you do not have to change yourself entirely for you to remove negative or destructive schemas from your system. You have the option of incorporating information into your existing knowledge, causing small but impactful adjustments in your life. However, if the schema requires a total transformation, then you have to prepare yourself to replace old beliefs and mindsets with new information that more accurately reflects the environment you live in.

Chapter 3 – How Does Schema Affect Our Decision-Making Process?

In general, the brain is the most complex and wondrous organ of the body. However, despite its many defenses, it remains vulnerable to several factors, rendering it imperfect at times. You might forget that you have an upcoming important appointment with a client and only remember it upon the last minute. You might have also committed an obvious mistake on your paper, making you feel incredibly foolish for overlooking that one detail. In some cases, such errors could even have harmful or even fatal repercussions to you and those around you.

Because the process of making a decision is

centered primarily in the brain, various factors also affect the quality of the decision and the efficiency of the process itself. Recognizing these factors is an important step in assuring that you are not simply being affected by certain schemas instead of making a rational decision based on the whole picture.

Before delving into the strategies on how to improve and safeguard your decision-making process, you must understand first how the brain can be tricked. In this chapter, you will learn:

1. Why the mind prefers taking shortcuts;
2. How you can be swayed by certain cognitive biases;

3. Why people tend to play the blame
   game for almost every situation;

4. How changes in one's self, the others,
   and the environment can blindside the
   brain; and

5. How flawed the human memory can be.

These points will be covered in the following
sections about the principles of stereotypes,
prejudice, and cognitive biases.

Stereotype

A set of pre-defined characteristics to a group
of people leads to the formation of
stereotypes. According to experts,
stereotypes do serve a practical purpose in

terms of how one interacts with the surrounding people. Since nearly every mental process at work during social interactions, the human mind creates and follow shortcuts that would allow them to initiate conversations, interpret the meanings behind each word and gesture, and respond appropriately.

Stereotypes are mostly based on characteristics that are visible or can easily be associated with a particular group. For this reason, people of color, women, and certain nationalities are more frequently stereotyped compared to others. It should be noted that stereotypes are not only negative traits.

Positive stereotypes also exist, such as when many people assume that African Americans are natural athletes.

The persistence and promulgation of stereotypes happen because humans are hard-wired to accept them. In a sense, stereotypes help unite the understanding and expectations of people towards a certain group. However, being on the receiving end of a stereotype can be quite a quite disturbing experience. Most stereotyped people face injustices and unfair treatment, just because the people around them have incorrect assumptions about their gender, color, or race, among others.

Stereotypes can also be passed around within and between communities. For instance, men assign stereotypes to women, and women stereotype men back. When either of the two begin to push more their respective stereotypes of the other group, an imbalance begins to form, which then only causes the two groups to drift further apart. This phenomenon can be observed between different racial groups. One infamous example of this in effect is the South African apartheid system that segregated the Caucasians from Africans residing in that country during the latter half of the 20th century.

It should be noted that stereotypes go beyond gender, color and race. Think back about your conversations with others about the people from the other city or the employees who belong to another department in the company you work for. Even sports fans teams are assigned stereotypes depending on how they support their respective favorite teams or athletes.

How Positive Stereotypes Weaken Your Judgment

Stereotypes are bad for your mental processes, regardless of whether they are positive or negative in nature. No two individuals are completely alike. Therefore, labelling a whole group of people with the characteristics possessed by only some of its members is terribly dehumanizing.

Though positive stereotypes are few and far in between, many people are unaware that they have them at all. This is primarily because most stereotypes present people in a negative light. Relying on positive stereotypes can also lead you to disappointment. You might believe that a particular group possesses a certain good quality. However, upon personally meeting someone from the said group who lacks that quality, you are likely to become disappointed with that person rather than realize that you had the wrong assumptions all along.

Take, for example, the following positive stereotypes about homosexual men. Due to how they are usually portrayed in different forms of media, many people believe that gay men are:

- In good physical shape;
- Always dressed fashionably;
- Friendly and affectionate;
- Outgoing; or
- Keenly interested in shopping.

If you do not know or have met a homosexual man before, you might assume that they would easily befriend you, or always be ready to go out at a moment's notice. You might also be inclined to ask them for fashion advice or tips on how to decorate well your new home. Such stereotypes—though the qualities per se are not necessarily negative— sets you up to having unrealistic expectations about gay men.

In the process, depending on the given positive stereotypes erase the fact that gay men are just like everybody else. They are separate individuals with different aspirations, interests, and personalities. Not all gay men are the epitome of physical fitness. Their sexual orientation does not have a direct link between how they prioritize exercising and eating a balanced diet. Many pursue careers in other fields aside from fashion, interior decoration, or event planning. As such, they are not meant to be anybody's shopping buddy or confidante.

When put in this manner, do you not think that labeling all gay men as such and such sounds ridiculous? In fact, categorizing people into boxes of qualities that they should all have is something that you should avoid at all costs. To further highlight this point, examine the following common positive stereotypes that people may have about women:

- All women are natural caretakers and therefore are good mothers as well.

- Every woman is more deserving of respect compared to men.
- A woman is naturally in touch with her emotions.

At first glance, it may seem that these statements can be nothing more than praises given to women in general. However, take apart each one of them and consider them as generalizations rather compliments. For example, many people believed that women should inherently act in a motherly manner. If a child is crying, most people expect women to pacify the crying child. Even if a man is physically closer to the said child than a woman, he likely believes that it is the duty of the woman to tend to it.

However, not all women like children. Some even hate interacting with them. Nowadays, it is no longer unheard of for women to refuse the idea of having children with their partners. As such, when a child cries while they are present, they do not naturally have the urge to calm the child down. Therefore, it is nice to assume that all women are good at taking care of others. However, it is wrong to assume that all women desire to be—and are meant to be—mothers.

It may also sound nice to assume that women are more deserving of others' respect compared to men. However, consider this following scenario. A father decides to stay at home to take care of the children while the mother works throughout the day. In this example, does the mother deserve more respect than the father simply because she is a woman? Does their living arrangement decrease the value of the father's contribution to the wellness of their family? If the situation is reversed, do you automatically respect only the father for working rather than staying at home with the kids? If you have answered yes to any of these questions, then you are exhibiting signs of possessing stereotypical beliefs about respect and gender roles.

Prejudice

When one believes that he or she is inherently better—but without solid proof—than a certain group of people, that person is demonstrating prejudicial attitudes and beliefs. Based on the word's Latin roots "prae" and "judicum", prejudice involves judging people before even getting to know them in a deeper and more comprehensive way.

As such, prejudices are not based on one's actual experiences with the said group of individuals. Rather, it is borne out of poor thoughts and negative assumptions that you have against someone. In addition, when prejudice remained uncorrected for a period, it can serve as the starting point for discriminatory acts that can be unfair and even fatal to everyone involved.

Differentiating Prejudice from Stereotypes and Discrimination

Many people tend to use interchangeably the terms "stereotype", "prejudice", and "discrimination" in their day-to-day conversations. Media sometimes commit this error as well and further confusing those who are not familiar with this topic. To clarify the differences between these terms, here are the salient points to remember about each term.

1. Stereotypes pertain to ideas or concepts that oversimplify or generalize a particular group of people. A stereotype can either be positive or negative towards the individual being stereotyped upon by others. Regardless, stereotypes do not fully encompass the complexities of every group, and as such, can lead people to make incorrect, and sometimes harmful, assumptions and decisions that affect everyone involved.

2. Prejudice comes in the form of subjective opinions, feelings and attitudes that are not reasonable or based on sound logic. Directed towards specific groups of people, prejudice is typically caused by a belief that certain groups are inherently better or worse than the others.

3. Discrimination involves a direct or indirect action from an individual as a result of the stereotypes and prejudices held by the said individual. Acts of discrimination normally cause significant damage on the affected person, whether on a physical, mental, emotional or even financial terms.

When you categorize people based on your personal expectations and feelings, you are running the risk of having your judgment affected in a way that could be harmful to those around you. More often than not, many people do not even realize that they are stereotyping someone, expressing their prejudicial beliefs, or committing acts of discrimination. They may simply be caught in their own versions of reality, when in fact, their thoughts and actions are only reinforcing the injustice and inequalities within their respective communities.

Common Types of Prejudice

Throughout history, cases of prejudice can be found among different social and cultural groups. As such, those on the receiving end have suffered—or for some, continues to suffer—from discrimination and oppression. Here is a list of prejudicial beliefs and how each affects one's decisions and behaviors.

Racism

This form of prejudice stems from the belief that all members of a particular nationality or socio-ethnic group possess the same qualities and abilities that are normal, and sometimes wrongly attributed to the said group. A racist mindset is also exhibited when the person believes that the traits, talents, and flaws of different nationalities or ethnic groups are because of the genetic differences between them. Basically, if one believes that a particular group of people is genetically superior or inferior compared to others, that person is racist.

Racial profiling, for instance, is a particularly sore point for people of color in the many predominantly white countries. This occurs when the law authorities automatically assume that a person has committed a crime based solely on his or her skin color. Such error in judgment has not only led to injustice and unfair treatment but also to the death of many individuals who were only at the wrong place and at the wrong time.

Nationalism and Xenophobia

Though sometimes equated with racism, nationalism is not a form of prejudice when demonstrated in positive and constructive manners. However, when taken to the extreme—and then combined with xenophobia, or the irrational fear of people from other countries—one's patriotic thoughts and feelings can turn into something that are more dangerous and hateful.

Essentially, nationalism becomes bad when people begin to adapt beliefs that immigrants and refugees are inferior to them, or are damaging to their respective communities, both without having any solid proof of such claims. This type of prejudice has long been observed across cultures and nations. Fearing the arrival of strangers from another land has caused death and destruction for both the locals and the immigrants. However, this fact does not stop this hurtful mindset from prevailing nowadays.

Reports of xenophobic instances continue to litter the front page. Most of them involving the following groups of people: immigrants from Middle Eastern countries, refugees from Syria, and immigrants from Latin America.

Classism

Basing one's opinions and behaviors on the socio-economic or social class of the people around them is the hallmark of classism. These classes can either be pre-determined by the society itself to which the said individual belongs to, or it can be merely self-determined by one's perceptions of social norms and expectations.

For example, certain people who have come from a privileged background tend to have negative opinions about those who live in poverty. This point of view is typically caused by associating every impoverished person with the crimes and other acts of violence that are usually reported to have happened in poor communities.

Some governments permit classism to persist, especially when such a mindset is deeply ingrained in the culture of their people. When this happens, those who belong in the upper or ruling class are granted complete or partial control over the quality of lives that lower classes could have. They could also try to limit the chances of others moving up through the classes by suppressing the opportunities that others might have. For instance, the ruling class decides to allocate government budgets to the beautification of their country rather than improving the current education system. Such an act sends out a signal from them that those of the lower classes do not deserve a high quality of education.

Ageism

This form of prejudice can affect both the younger generations and the older people. Rather than viewing them as individuals, those with ageist views believe that all members of the same age group think and behave in the same manner. Because of this, certain rights, privileges, and understanding can be unreasonably withheld from the young or the old.

Young people, for instance, might be disallowed by their communities to participate in discussions about policies and legislations that directly affect them. The likely cause for this that the given community does not believe that people below a particular age could contribute to arguments against or support for the decision that is going to be made.

It could also be a case of failing to recognize the capability of youths to understand well enough their wants and needs as individuals.

Whatever the reason may be, the exclusion of young people from key discussions that affect them is a definite demonstration of ageist beliefs.

On the other hand, the elderly living in a care facility tend to be refused access to technology, such as the Internet and mobile apps. In such cases, the caretakers are assuming that old people cannot be taught or cannot learn on their own the ins and outs of using new technology. As such, they cannot be bothered to assist the elderly in exploring their interest with social media platforms, mobile entertainment, and other helpful apps that are specifically designed to aid those in their advanced ages.

Sexism

Though more commonly directed towards women, sexism can be observed happening to both men and women. In general, sexist views manifest due to the belief that one of the given sexes is more superior, completely or partially, than the other. Even though members of either sexes excel in a given field, this type of prejudice persists among people who believe that such instances are outliers rather than proofs that their sexist opinions are wrong.

Looking through the history and current status of many nations, women are treated as intellectually and emotionally inferior compared to men. As such, certain rights like voting and property ownership are deprived from them. Furthermore, the belief that women are inferior beings propagate acts of violence and discrimination towards them within the home, at the workplace, and within the community they belong to. Being viewed as inherently emotional, women who report such cases are undermined by their peers and authorities in terms of the accuracy and personal impact of their claims.

On the other hand, sexism among men occurs when a man exhibits behavior or expresses thoughts that are not considered as manly attributes. For example, men who are inherently more emotional than others are labeled immediately as either effeminate or weak. Since being open about one's emotion is viewed as a feminine trait, a man crying over something trivial or significant might be prejudiced against by his peers.

Men pursuing careers or professions that are normally associated with women are likely to be receivers of sexism in the workplace. For instance, childcare services have always been a field dominated by women. Because of this, some employers feel uncomfortable or downright repulsed by the idea of having a man as a nanny for their children.

Homophobia or Anti-LGBT Prejudice

Non-binary gendered individuals have long faced prejudice against their preferences and behaviors. Because such beliefs are deeply ingrained in many societies, discriminative policies have been passed, thereby significantly affecting the rights, privileges, and quality of life of those who belong to the LGBT community.

For instance, a much-debated topic upon is a restriction on marriage imposed upon couples who are not in a heterosexual relationship.

Homosexuals, bisexuals, and transgendered people tend to be viewed as promiscuous by society. As such, opinions on how they would preserve the sanctity of marriage and familial relationships are being put forward and used as support for legislations that prohibit them from marrying their respective partners.

Transgender, in particular, are oppressed not only in legal terms. They are frequently subjected to derision and violence from other members of the community, simply out of fear that transgendered individuals would be allowed to use bathrooms assigned to the gender to which they identify themselves to.

Religious Prejudice

Basing your hatred, uneasiness, or contempt on a person's religious affiliation and beliefs indicates that you are exhibiting signs of religious prejudice towards that said person. This frequently happens when the leaders and/or literature of a given religion cultivate the idea that those who do not follow the same religion as they do are heathens. As a result, conflict and violence occur between two or more religious groups, turning their prejudice into discrimination.

People who have a prejudice towards other religions tend to believe that the religion they belong to is the only true faith that everyone must believe in as well. This total conviction of their superiority causes them to dismiss other religions as nothing more than groups that either need to be converted or eliminated.

Throughout the history of the world, wars have been waged between and within nations in the name of their gods and religions. Loss and destruction of lives and properties were just some horrific results of people giving in to the pull of the prejudices they held. Some examples of infamous holy wars include the Crusades—a series of military expeditions in the 11th, 12th, and 13th century, wherein many European Christians endeavored to recover their holy land from Muslims.

Aside from wars, religious prejudice can be observed happening in the workplace. There have been many reports of employers refusing to hire someone just because the applicant is from a religion that they do not agree with. Some employees have complained about the respective companies they are working for due to the active suppression of opportunities to practice their religion. In extreme cases, religious differences have led coworkers to fight and hurt one another while on duty.

Nowadays, religious prejudice has also tainted the politics and societal norms of many countries. As such, they use these irrational beliefs to support policies and regulations that discriminate against certain religions. If you are keeping up with the news, many people from the US are vocal about implementing laws that would ban the entry of Muslims into their country, believing that every Muslim is a possible terrorist who wishes to destroy US in the name of their religion. Statistics, however, show that the likelihood of terrorists slipping by the inspections by blending in with the tourists and immigrants is significantly low. Still, because of their deep-seated prejudices, people with such beliefs refuse to acknowledge their irrationality and change their mindsets for the better. Other high-profile examples that still dominate the newsfeed every now and then include the conflicts between the Hindus, Sikhs, and Muslims living in India, and the suppression of Buddhist Tibetans by controlling, but powerful Chinese government.

Disability Prejudice

Negative opinions and attitudes towards disabled individuals remain common, even in this age of political correctness. A person who has these prejudicial beliefs automatically view people with physical or mental disabilities as weak and less deserving of the opportunities, rights, and privileges normally afforded to the rest of their community. As such, discriminative policies and rules are created and passed without much consideration of the needs and lives of disabled people.

In extreme cases, societies and even governments tried to force the sterilization of disabled individuals, citing studies that indicate the genetic factors of passing on disabilities to the next generation. Another common example of this prejudice in effect can be observed during the selection process of qualified applicants for a given job. Due to the belief that their physical or mental conditions make them weaker than the rest, people with disabilities tend to be overlooked by the selection committee, even if they possess the required skills and qualifications for the said job.

Some prejudicial beliefs are not as harmful as the ones given above. A person is exhibiting an ableist prejudice when he or she believes that all disabled people need to have their own caretakers all the time. There are also people who fail to understand that disabilities are relatively common in any society. As a result, they do not see the importance of passing on laws and regulations that would be fair and reasonable to people with disabilities. Such prejudices may still be corrected if proper awareness would be raised about the needs and rights of physically or mentally disabled individuals.

How Prejudice Affects Decisions about One's Wellbeing

With the wide range of forms that it can take, prejudice significantly affects the lives of millions of people all around the world. Its scope is not limited to the societal level only. Instead, its effects can be felt deeply on a personal level by anyone who is on the receiving end of a prejudice. As a result, one's judgement are impaired by inaccurate beliefs of others about them, thereby affecting other important areas of his or her life. After having surveyed different literature and studies conducted on this matter, here is a list of five negative effects of prejudice on one's physical, mental, social, and emotional wellbeing.

Poor Performance

A study reveals that people who have been exposed to stereotypes and prejudices held by others about the group they belong to are likely to live up to the poor expectations assigned to them. Experts call this phenomenon "stereotype threat," and its effects cross boundaries between genders, race, and religious beliefs.

Further studies show that when a member of a minority group receives a reminder of any prejudice about their said group, the quality of his or her performance tends to suffer greatly. To demonstrate this, here is an experiment conducted among a set of women participants with similar academic performances. Those in the experimental group were exposed to literature that claimed that men are better than women at solving math problems. The control group, on the other hand, did not receive any priming from the researchers. After a while, both groups were asked to take standardized mathematical tests. Upon checking the results of the exams, those who belonged in the experimental group scored significantly lower compared to their peers assigned to the control group.

In the example given above, the women who were reminded of their supposed inferiority performed according to the expectations that have been set for them. Despite having the same amount of education and similar levels of abilities, the prejudiced group failed to maintain or keep up with the performance exhibited by those who were not exposed to the said prejudice.

Some studies also show that stereotype threat can be particularly potent for some people. In such cases, they do not need to be explicitly reminded of their assumed weaknesses. Just drawing the attention to the race or gender they belong to—for instance, asking the test-takers to indicate if they are male or female on the response sheet—is enough to trigger the negative effects of being prejudiced upon by society in general.

Increased Vulnerability to Physical Illnesses and Diseases

It should not come as a surprise that prejudice creates highly stressful environments and situations for those who experience it. Therefore, because of the elevated stress levels, prejudiced people are likely to develop previously identified illnesses and diseases that are linked to stress, such as different forms of congenital problems, stroke, various types of cancers, and diabetes, among others.

One study conducted in 2008 indicate that the health disparities that exist between Caucasian Americans and African Americans may be correlated to racial tension and inequality. According to statistical data on hand, Caucasian American men tend to live for around seven years more than African American men. In addition, those in racial minority groups are more likely to develop stress-related chronic illnesses. Though there is no direct link connecting stress, race, and prejudice at the moment, researchers suggest that further studies may reveal exactly how prejudice could affect one's physical health.

Development or Worsening of Mental Health Problems

Stress does not only wreak havoc on one's body. It can also cause or agitate existing mental conditions that a person has. As one study indicates, there are significantly more women who are suffering from acute anxiety compared to men. Similarly, women develop post-traumatic stress disorders more than twice as much as men do. Although there are various contributing factors to the decline of one's mental health, experts agree that prejudice and discriminatory acts have large impacts on making a person feel even more mentally vulnerable.

Substance Abuse

According to the data released by the US agency assigned to administer and monitor health services to those who abuse drugs and other addictive substances, the cost of their expenses is significantly higher among those in the minority groups. Furthermore, a 2010 study on women who abuses drug show that those feel prejudiced upon are more likely to succumb to the temptation of hard substances. It is believed that the stress of receiving prejudicial thoughts and discriminatory acts has partially led those women to look for ways to escape from their realities.

Formation of Self-Sabotaging Behaviors

People who experience frequent bouts of self-doubt over their poor performances tend to have lowered self-esteem as well. In order to cope with such situations, some people turn to self-sabotaging behaviors. For instance, a student who wishes to pass the entrance exam to a prestigious university feels anxious about his chances to make it through this stage of selection. Rather than dwell on his worries, he decides to go out and drink the night before the test so that in case he fails, he can blame his low scores to a hangover.

Among people who belong to prejudiced groups, this phenomenon can be observed whenever they try to cope with their realities by committing to damaging behaviors and addictions. A woman who feels prejudiced and discriminated upon in the workplace might feel like the need to imbibe alcohol on a regular basis just to feel less of her suffering at work. Eventually, her personal life and work performance would also suffer due to her growing dependence on alcohol, thus fulfilling the negative expectations that some people around her have about career women.

As evidenced by the studies cited above, prejudice can mold the target's perception of how the world works, how other people regard him or her, and how one feels about himself or herself as an individual. More importantly, prejudices can also influence how the person thinks about his or her future. Some might be discouraged when faced with the injustices of the world. They might assume that no matter how much they improve, the people around them would just always reduce their achievements based on the prejudices against them.

To correct this line of thinking, it is not enough to uplift the views of those who are prejudiced about themselves, other people, and the world in general. Those who also hold prejudices against certain groups of people must also realize the errors in their thoughts and attitudes and be open to changes that would improve their negative and weak mental models of others. Only them would the effects of prejudice be mitigated among those who suffer the burdens of being dehumanized and belittled every single day.

Cognitive Bias

Systematic errors in your thought processes are commonly caused by various forms of cognitive biases. In general, anything that can affect the decisions and judgement that you make are considered as biases that you possess about the reality of the environment you belong to, and the people around you.

As explained earlier, the brain can be influenced by a wide range of factors that are either within or outside the person's control. For instance, an influx of information can lead the brain to oversimplify the process of interpreting the large volume of presented information. In some cases, failure to pay attention to critical details of an event can color the way the person recalls the said event later on.

Not all cognitive biases are inherently bad, however. Some psychologists argue that humans rely on certain biases in order to adapt to the environment and speed up the decision-making process. Making a quick, impulsive decision instead of a slow but deliberate decision can spell out the difference between life and death on some occasions.

For example, walking down a darkened alley could bring up your cognitive biases about the dangers of being alone in such an area. As a result, you try your hardest to reach the end of the alley and get back to the main street where you would feel somewhat safer from potential muggers. Though you have no proof, that danger is literally waiting for you behind the shadows, the red alerts ringing inside your brain have brought you quicker to a decision that could save you from harmful or even fatal situations

Common Types of Cognitive Biases

Though you might think that your thoughts are logical and rational all the time, the unfortunate fact is that cognitive biases influence everyone in little and significant ways. Depending on the type of bias, a person's mental processes can be distorted, thereby affecting both one's judgments and decisions.

There are various forms that cognitive biases can take. Some are fairly obvious, while some are nearly impossible to notice. To help you identify them, here is a list of the ten common types of cognitive biases that affect your thoughts, feelings, and behaviors.

The Actor-Observer Bias

How one perceives the people around him or her depends on a wide range of factors. However, researchers have reported that one of the heavier influences among these variables hinges upon whether the person is an actor or an observer for a given situation.

According to their studies, if a person is the actor, he or she would typically practice an external attribution. For example, you might excuse your failure to pass an exam because of the tricky nature of the questions designed by your teacher.

On the other hand, explaining the actions of those around you is likely to be attributed to internal factors. If you have a tendency to think your classmates who screw up the exam are either lazy or stupid, you are exhibiting signs of an actor-observer bias. Compared to your reasoning from before, you did not take into account the trick questions that you have failed at answering correctly as well.

The Anchoring Bias

People tend to be heavily influenced by the first information that they get about a particular topic. For example, the first amount of money offered during a negotiation usually becomes the anchoring point for the rest of the counteroffers that will be made during the entirety of the given transaction.

This cognitive bias is not limited only two numbers, though this is more frequently observed in situations that are number-based. Unfortunately, doctors are one of the most commonly affected by this distortion. When making their diagnosis, their first impressions are typically turned into anchoring points that influence their subsequent assessments.

This is also notably prevalent among doctors who prefer to ask their patients to recount the entirety of their medical history rather than rely on records. More often than not, only when a specialist tries to narrow down the root-cause of the medical problem can the effects of anchoring bias be diminished or eliminated.

The Availability Heuristic

A person's tendency to believe that something is likely to happen due to the number of examples one can think of readily is a type of cognitive bias known as the availability heuristic. Experts on human development believe that many people rely on this mental shortcut to give themselves a quicker assessment of the risks involved by engaging in a particular activity.

For example, there are many people who cite the likelihood of a plane crash as the reason for their fear of flying. Since unfortunate incidents involving airplanes are given more attention in the news than car accidents, many people are led to believe that air travel is far more dangerous than traveling by land. Statistics on the safety of different types of transportation, however, indicate otherwise.

Though it may seem relatively harmless at first glance, this cognitive bias can usually lead to one committing bad decisions and poor calculations. Smokers who do not personally know anyone who has died of smoking-related complications tend to overlook the growing number of people who suffer from lung or throat cancer.

The Confirmation Bias

You can observe a person influenced by confirmation bias when he or she has a tendency to listen and accept only information that are aligned with the thoughts and beliefs that they already have. When presented with two arguments from opposing sides of the issues, this person favors the argument that confirms his or personal opinion about the given issue.

This particular bias is frequently exhibited by people who engage in discussions about global warming and gun control—two of the most polarizing issues across the world. Rather than listening to what the other side has to say and reviewing all the facts in an objective and rational manner, people usually consider only the information that strengthens what they already believe to be true.

In a smaller scale, confirmation bias is at work when two persons walk away with different interpretations of the same story. Each person picked only points of the story that validate their beliefs and points of view. As such, when asked about the story, their recollection becomes distorted by their personal filters and opinions.

The False Consensus Effect

Many people are observed to exhibit a tendency to form too high of an estimate about the number of individuals who are in agreement with their thoughts, values, behaviors, and attitudes. Known as the false consensus effect, this form of cognitive bias causes people to overestimate the value of their personal opinions.

According to studies conducted about this, people fall victim to this for two simple reasons. First, people tend to spend a majority of their time with family and friends who most likely share the same beliefs and points of view. As a result, a person would start to believe that his or her own thought about a particular subject is shared among a large amount of people. Even when in the company of people who are in disagreement with the said opinion, some people still fail to realize the error in their ways of thinking.

The second probable reason is the human tendency to feel better whenever someone agrees with one's thoughts and emotions. If this does not come naturally for a given person, he or she might be inclined to recreate these feelings by believing that others share their opinions, even without having any hard proof of such a thing. On some level, they benefit from this cognitive bias by gaining a boost for their self-esteem and a sense of belongingness.

The Halo Effect

One of the studies on human cognition indicates that students tend to rate attractive professors as more competent, kinder, and funnier compared to their less good-looking counterparts. This distortion in one's perception is caused by a type of cognitive bias called the halo effect.

Rooted on the principle of "what is beautiful must be good", this cognitive bias has a massive influence in everyone's day-to-day life. Turn on the TV and observe the commercials of different products. More often than not, the product or service is being promoted by a young, fit, and charming model with a grin from ear to ear. Imagine the same product being endorsed by a gloomy, repulsive person. Which one do you think would be more effective at enticing you to go out and buy yourself that product? Aside from commercials, the halo effect can also be observed in a work environment.

According to studies, a well-dressed job applicant who has a pleasing personality is believed by many interviewers to be more qualified for the job in comparison to another applicant who has the same credentials but lack the other candidate's level of attractiveness.

The Hindsight Bias

The tendency to view events—random or planned—as predictable instances is caused by one's hindsight bias. If a person claims that he or she has "known it all along", there is a high likelihood that the person is experiencing this particular cognitive bias. For example, after taking an exam, students like to go over the questions that they find difficult. At this point, some students might think that they knew the right answer all along, but only chose the wrong option out of hesitation caused by some other reason. However, more often than not, they have gotten the question wrong because they did not actually know the correct answer while they were taking the test. They only think they knew it because others have said so after the test is already over.

People who invest in stocks also tend to believe that they could have predicted where the trend is heading to, when in fact, they do not have any sort of prior information or research that could have served as a basis for such claims. Even when they lose money for making the wrong move, some would still claim that they knew the high risks involved for doing so. Without proof, such accounts are likely incidences of hindsight bias going into effect.

The Misinformation Effect

Researchers have noted that human memory can be significantly influenced by events that have transpired right after the moment when a given memory has been created. This phenomenon is called the misinformation effect.

An experiment conducted by Elizabeth Loftus shows how this distortion in one's memory could happen. In her study, she made her subjects view a video of a car crash. She then divided them into two and asked similar questions save for one detail. To the first group, she asked about their perception about the speed of each car when they "hit" one another. On the other hand, she asked the second group about the speed of the cars when they "smashed" into each other.

After one week, Loftus' group presented a follow-up question to each group. When asked if the car crash resulted to a spray of broken glass, participants from the second group were noted to be more likely to affirm seeing this happening compared to those from the first group. Because of the slight difference between the wording of the first set of questions, a false memory about the car crash has been subtly planted among some participants of the experiment.

The Optimism Bias

Many people tend to think in more optimistic terms, sometimes to a fault. It is good to be positive about things that are going in your life. However, overestimating the likelihood of having a good fortune can lead you to being blindsided by negative events that could significantly affect your life. For instance, some people live in a bubble for so long that they do not know what to do when illness, divorce, or death of a loved one suddenly becomes a part of their life.

Unrealistic optimism can have a devastating impact on one's day-to-day life. In some cases, it has led people to take risks that should have been avoided all along, such as driving a car without putting the seatbelt on or drinking themselves to a stupor every weekend.

Research shows that optimism bias is quite hard to eliminate from one's system. The good news, however, is that relying on this cognitive bias makes one more hopeful of their future. They become more motivated to achieve their respective goals. Therefore, even though it can be fatal at times, optimism bias remains a gray area for most cognitive psychologists.

The Self-Serving Bias

One of the hardest mental distortions to recognize by yourself is the self-serving bias. Essentially, people have a tendency to credit themselves for favorable outcomes. On the other hand, failures are usually blamed for some other reasons other than their personal capabilities and actions.

For instance, a student believes that he has done well in an exam because he has prepared well for it. However, when the same student fails to get good marks for a project, he blames his luck or some other circumstances that may or may not have anything to do with the said project.

According to some experts, self-serving bias does have a positive effect on a person's mental health. It can serve as a buffer to protect one's level of self-esteem. However, in most cases, indulging yourself in this type of bias can lead you to blame the people around you for your own shortcoming. As a result, you would end up not learning from your mistakes, which could then cause the recurrence of the same problem—or a more intense version of it—later on.

Why Cognitive Biases Persist

Essentially, humans rely on certain cognitive biases because they do help in addressing the four problematic areas of interaction with others and the environment they belong to. To get a holistic understanding of your cognitive biases, examine them in light of the following issues that you might be experiencing regularly.

Problem #1: Information Overload

The reality of your environment can bombard you with too much information. Because of this, you are usually left with no option but to filter out most of what you are supposed to sensing and perceiving. The brain is hard-wired to pick up information that would likely be of use for you later on. However, this process can be influenced by several factors, such as

<u>Repetition</u>

Humans remember more about things that have been repeated over and over again. For example, the frequency illusion or also known as the Baader-Meinhof phenomenon happens when you seemingly start seeing everywhere something that you have just recently learned or noticed. As such, the information becomes more ingrained into one's memory, thereby letting it be retained as a part of one's knowledge or a long-term memory.

<u>Unusual or surprising qualities</u>
The importance of an information increases when it possesses a trait that one considers as either strange, funny or striking. Things that are expected or normal tend to be skipped over by the brain.

As exhibited by the bizarreness effect, people tend to remember strange information because its quality makes it more distinctive than the rest of the available information.

Changes

Whether the change is positive or negative, a person tends to examine and evaluate the changes they perceive about a certain thing. This can also happen when two previously similar things appear to become different upon the next viewing.

A cognitive bias called the framing effect illustrates how a person's perception can be changed depending on whether an information has been presented in a positive or negative manner. For example, highlighting the profits and gains of a business rather than the operational expenses make the said business seem more attractive to potential investors.

Flaws of Others

People tend to be blind about their own flaws since they are more drawn about the flaws committed by other people. Some people even point out flaws in others without realizing that they themselves possess the same or similar flaws as well. Naïve cynicism, for example, occurs when people assume that those who are in disagreement with their opinions automatically exhibit egocentric biases. In contrast, naïve realism, another form of cognitive bias, is at play when one believes that any other point of view that is not objective should be considered as biased or irrational.

Similarity with Existing Beliefs

In general, a person tends to ignore information that does not align with one's currently held beliefs about something. Aside from confirmation bias, this can also be observed among researchers who are under the influence of the expectation bias, or also referred to as the observer-expectancy effect. In such cases, the researcher projects his or her own biases onto the participants of an experiment, thereby influencing how the results of the study would be interpreted.

Problem #2: Incomplete Information

In order to survive, humans have to make do with whatever information they have about the world. After all, the brain can only handle a certain amount of information at a given time. As such, the mind automatically limits the flow of information, sometimes leaving out key pieces of information that one has no choice but to fill out on his or her own. Connecting the dots with the aid of cognitive biases are achieved by:

<u>Searching for patterns and context clues</u>
Since no one ever has the complete set of information at all times, the brain has to

compensate for it by imagining what could have gone in between each set of information.

This process is vulnerable towards the effects of various types of cognitive biases, such as the anecdotal fallacy—or the tendency to refer to a personal experience or isolated instances as viable replacements for logical argument and solid evidences.

Relying on stereotypes and prior knowledge
Mental gaps are usually filled out by the set of related information you already have, regardless of whether or not they are accurate. Because of this, many tend to forget which parts are true and which parts have

been conveniently filled in by generalities and one's personal knowledge of the subject matter.

Automation bias, for example, happens whenever one favors using stereotypes and generalizations as references during the process of making decisions, ignoring any detail that would offer contradictory information, even if it is proven to be more accurate than one's beliefs and ideas.

<u>Viewing familiar or pleasant persons and objects in a more positive light</u>
Human perception tends to be colored by one's level of familiarity or attraction towards

a particular person or object. High levels tend to automatically skew your perception of someone or something towards favorable. Therefore, lower levels can cause a person to dislike someone or something even without fully knowing the reason behind such a reaction.

The most widely observed cognitive bias that fits this description is the halo effect, wherein perception and interpretation of information is distorted by one's positive regard and good impression of the other person or event.

The subconscious mind of humans is not naturally good at anything related to math. This means that if there is missing information about digits or probabilities, the likelihood of making an error exponentially increases.

This can be observed with the so-called money illusion, or also known as the price illusion. Since modern currency has no intrinsic value whatsoever, thinking of money in nominal terms only prevents the person from considering the more important factor to consider—the purchasing power of money vis-à-vis the current economic environment that a person is in at a given moment.

Assuming one knows how others think

Some tend to believe that their thoughts reflect those of others. This happens whenever one tries to model others after one's self. However, the fact is that no two humans think exactly alike at all times.

You may have experienced being in this situation when you believe that the attention of everyone nearby is centered on you. This phenomenon is called the spotlight effect, and as proven by studies, it is rarely, if ever, an accurate account of one's current situation.

<u>Projecting one's attitudes and assumptions</u>

This is similar to the assumption of having like minds with others, except this one factors in the time that has gone since the event has happened, or the changes that could happen during the time that would pass by. For example, outcome bias occurs when one evaluates the quality of a decision—made either personally, or by another person—after the outcome of the said decision has already been realized.

Problem #3: The Need to Think Effectively yet Efficiently

Without the capability to think on one's feet, humans would have long been wiped out as a species. As people go through the day, most try their best to process every bit of information that would get through their respective filters. However, everyone is constrained by time as well because taking too much of it to analyze everything can lead to inaction and lost opportunities. In order to act in time and accordingly, a person has to:

<u>Have confidence in one's importance and ability to make a significant impact</u>

Without self-confidence, a person may not have the needed boost to act as quickly as the situation requires. However, in some cases, some people tend to overshoot, making them feel overly confident instead.

As an effect, one may experience the effects of optimism bias, wherein a person believes that a negative event is not likely happen to them, even if he or she had not done anything to prevent its occurrence. This cognitive bias is also referred to as "comparative optimism" or "unrealistic optimism".

<u>Focus on short-term goals rather than long-term plans</u>

To figure out the next move, humans tend to prioritize whatever is happening in the present instead of what would happen in the long run. Many are also inclined to act on something that they could see the effects immediately compared to things that require one's capacity to appreciate delayed gratification.

This is what happens to people who experience cognitive bias called the appeal to novelty. In such cases, a person is likely to believe that a certain idea is automatically better or correct simply because it is new information that seemingly conforms to modern standards rather than tradition.

<u>Be motivated enough to finish things that one has already started doing</u>

Much like the first law of motion by Sir Isaac Newton, an action that has been put into motion stays in motion. This is the principle behind a person's persistence to push through an endeavor, even in the face of one obstacle after another.

For instance, someone who has experienced the escalation of commitment can tell you that he or she could not seem to get out of an investment even if things have gone downhill.

Avoid making a decision that can no longer be taken back after it has been made

When faced with a set of options, a person tends to select the one that seems the least risky or the one that might preserve the existing state of affairs. Others face tough situations that are familiar to them rather than take a chance on unpredictable scenarios.

This is exemplified by several types of cognitive biases such as the law of instrument—or also known as the law of the hammer, the golden hammer, or Maslow's gavel—the hippo problem, and the status quo bias. For example, people under the status quo bias tend to make emotion-based decisions that would maintain the current status of the situation.

<u>Focus on tasks that seem simple and straightforward instead of complex and vague ones</u>

People usually prioritize things that are doable at the moment rather than attempt to sort out a complicated issue, even if doing the latter would be a better use of one's resources in the long run. Such a tendency is clearly reflected by the law of triviality, or otherwise known as the bike-shed effect. This was first observed among members of an organization who made disproportionate arguments in support of trivial matters rather than the important agenda items for that particular meeting.

Problem #4: Uncertainty about Which Information Must Be Remembered for Later

Because there is literally too much information coming in your way, you can only keep the ones that might be useful for you in the future. Without even realizing it, everyone gambles and makes trade-offs on which information must be remembered and which can be forgotten.

Take, for example, the generalizations you have about certain groups of people. You might prefer to keep them rather than minute details about every single person you meet because they are easier to store in your memory, and because they do not take as much as space as the other option.

If the pieces of information cannot be reduced into generalities, a person might opt to remember only some details that standout and then ignore the rest. In such cases, whatever would be picked depends on the person's filters that are in place. This means that the process itself is self-reinforcing of what you already know at the moment. To better illustrate these points, here are the various brain activities that affect how one selects critical information that must be committed to memory for later use:

A. *Editing and strengthening only certain parts of the memory after the event has already transpired*

When a person processes an event that has happened to him or her, some details may be forgotten or swapped with a different information that completely changes the sequence of things. As a result, only certain parts of the original memory become stored for the long term, while the edited parts turn into a seemingly vague—but actually inaccurate—recollections later on. This can be observed during the phenomenon called the misattribution of memory. A person is exhibiting this when he or she can remember the details of the memory but, due to various factors, cannot correctly identify the true source of the said memory.

B. *Disposing of specific details to create generalities*

Due to the limited capacity of the brain to store information, people automatically reduce events or lists into a set of elements that capture only parts of the whole thing, but would be later treated as a representation of the whole thing.

As exhibited by the peak-end rule, people tend to remember the details that happened at the most intense part of an experience—or it peak—and the details that happened at the end of the said experience. Instead of considering the total or average of each moment, one refers to the peaks and ends only to describe a particular experience.

C. *Storing a memory differently based on how it was formed*

Instead of choosing which memory to store based on its value, the brain can be confounded into selecting bits that only seemed important at the given time. Several factors contribute to this, including whatever else is going on at the time of the memory encoding, and the manner on which each piece of information has been presented during the said event.

The Google Effect, or also known as digital amnesia, becomes known when researchers observe a growing tendency among Internet users to forget pieces of information that can be easily found online through the use of the search function of any given browser. Researchers suggest that because of the high availability of information, people do not make much of an effort to remember details that they can look up again, in case they need to recall them in the future.

You do not have to remember all these four significant problems of the brain that bring about one's dependence on cognitive biases. Just remember the following points in order to better understand yourself vis-à-vis the personal biases that could be coloring your decisions and judgment.

1. Due to an overload of information, the brain tends to aggressively filter out information until everything becomes manageable once more. At this point, the noises around you turn into signals.

2. Using whatever resources you have at the time, the brain tries to fill in

the gaps that have been left after it has filtered out some important pieces of information. The signals you have received earlier are processed in order to get the message that they are trying to convey.

3. You usually do not have the luxury of time to carefully think about your decisions, so you take the risk and jump into conclusions. During this step, the manner and speed of reading the messages influences the kind of decisions that you would make.

4. The brain can only store so much information until everything

becomes a jumble once more. Therefore, it tries to eliminate what seems to be unnecessary bits of information and only keeps the ones that might prove useful later on. Whatever is left shapes the mental models you have of yourself, the others, and the world.

Just by looking at these points, it may seem that using cognitive biases during the decision-making process is reasonable. However, believing this would leave you vulnerable to their downsides as well.

How Cognitive Biases Weaken Your Mental Models

Each of the following solutions offered by cognitive biases also comes with their respective disadvantages. The key to avoiding further problems, therefore, is gaining an awareness that you are taking shortcuts rather than making deliberate but sound decisions. Consider these four issues that stem from the over-usage of cognitive biases in one's day-to-day life.

1. You do not get to see everything.

Filters are beneficial for you if and only if they block out unnecessary information only. However, in most cases, people cannot adjust their filters accordingly, leading them to miss out key information that could be useful when it is time to make a decision.

2. Your search for meaning can lead you to illogical or even harmful assumptions.

Imagining how an event has transpired can quickly become a source of mistakes and bad judgments. You are essentially fabricating a story that fits only your point of view rather than the whole truth of the situation.

3. Decisions that are made too quickly tend to have serious flaws.

Rash decisions are usually self-serving since you did not have the opportunity to consider every side of the story. At times, they can also be counterproductive since, more often than not, they are partially or completely wrong.

4. Your memories can further strengthen the mental errors you have made.

The bits of information that you keep tend to conform to what you already have. This means that rather than expanding your mind, you are only reinforcing both the good and bad attitudes and beliefs you have about people, objects, and events, among others.

Given these, you can conclude that cognitive biases are just like any other that you may have at your disposal. When applied in the right context and with moderation, they can be quite useful and even life-saving at times. However, when abused, over-reliance on cognitive biases can create more problems and lead to further harm. The human brain is capable of achieving remarkable feats of ingenuity and resourcefulness. It also plays a vital role in the plans and decisions that you make for day-to-day life, such as remembering the conversations you have had with your friends and having a productive day at work with your colleagues.

Having confidence about your plans and decisions is a wonderful trait to possess. However, you should always keep in mind that the brain is far from perfect. Furthermore, there are times when you cannot entirely avoid every threat that could compromise the quality and speed of your decisions. Still, gaining an awareness of the many ways schemas could affect your decision-making is a critical part of developing yourself as a rational thinker.

The brain is indeed susceptible to being tricked. Fortunately, you are also capable of improving the important mental structures that serve as foundations of your thoughts,

attitudes, and behaviors.

Chapter 4 – Improve Your Mental Models

With the recent prominence of the cognitive behavioral sciences comes the rise of mental models as well. There are literally thousands of them now, but they are also not created equally. The mental models you currently hold are not the best for the goal in life that you want to achieve.

Identifying the mental models that you need to have can be a daunting task, given the multitude of options you have on your hands. To help you through this process, here are four mental models derived from different fields of interest that you may be able to apply into life and improve the way you think, decide, and act.

Mental Model in Economics: Gresham's Law

The principle of bad elements driving out the good elements from a system over time is what constitutes Gresham's Law.

Historical Background

As a financier during the Tudor reign in England, Sir Thomas Gresham explained that forged coins could replace the real coins as the instigators of forgery hoarded the latter and let the rest of population use the fake currency for transactions. Without any form of verification or checkpoints, no one but the culprits could immediately recognize the differences between the two types of coins.

The exact origin of this mental model, however, is contested by experts on cognitive science and mental models. Some believe that the concept behind Gresham's Law has been proposed earlier by Nicolaus Copernicus around forty years before Sir Thomas Gresham did. The latter only managed to be more successful in drawing the attention of more people into the existence of the problems caused by a bad coinage. As such, selected literature about this mental model refers to the principle as the Gresham-Copernicus' Law.

Still, there are researchers who believe that the earliest record of this issue about the circulation of fake currency is from Aristophanes, a playwright from ancient Greece. One of his plays highlights the similarities between the decay of great politicians with the introduction of bad coins into society.

In the modern days, the problem with fake currency has mostly been effectively addressed by banks and financial institutions. However, the problems that this situation causes remain significant enough to merit the legacy of Gresham's Law. The conclusion of

Aristophanes' play is reflected in the way humans succumb to the pressures of their peers and society as a whole. If a person adapts a destructive behavior, it is almost impossible to drive out that behavior as long as the person believes that he or she gets some sort of survival advantage or benefit out of the said behavior. In this way, Gresham's Law bears similarities with the principle of evolution by natural selection—wherein organisms that possess qualities that allow them to survive live on, while those that don't die out.

Gresham's Law in Action

The general rule is that if a behavior serves a practical and competitive purpose, it will take root and continue to be carried out until it has outlived its usefulness or until another superior behavior replaces it. Because of these organizations and individuals who are only interested in their betterment and interests are more likely to fall under the effects described by Gresham's Law. The only way to circumvent this is to establish control points and maintain a check-and-balance system. Otherwise, the bad but beneficial practices would drive out morality and ethics until the organization or individual has become fully corrupted.

For you to better visualize the effects of this principle, here are some sample scenarios on how bad could drive the good out of a system:

a. Anna and Rachel are competing medical technicians who work for the same company by selling a particular brand of anti-depressants.

Anna employs bribery as one of her primary strategies for making a sale. Though she has several tools under her belt that would help her convince doctors to choose her product, she has observed that bribing them is the most effective and efficient method. As such, she has no qualms about bribing doctors left and right just to reach her monthly sales target.

On the other hand, Rachel refuses to succumb to unethical practices of selling her product. She relies on her training as a salesperson and the network she has built over the years. Because of this, there are times where she struggles to meet the sales target, stressing her and her team leader as a result.

If the medical industry itself does not punish fraudulent selling tactics, and the company continues to prioritize profits over ethical business practices,

Anna would continue to maintain a sustainable advantage over Rachel. This advantage would further strengthen Anna's bad behavior since she will be rewarded with bonuses and promotions.

Over time, even if checkpoints become established in the system, Anna is not likely going to change her tactics. Instead, she would actively look for ways to continue bribing her way into selling anti-depressants to willing doctors.

b. During the 2008 financial crisis in the US stock market, experts believe that one of the causes of this meltdown is the sub-prime lending practices of institutions that provide mortgage lending services. Banks have always competed amongst each other over which one of them would be able to attract the number of borrowers. To protect themselves and the market itself, systems and standards are put into place. However, in the process of gaining an advantage over the others, a significant number of banks had allowed their standards to slide down to zero.

Failing to realize that it would become a losing endeavor in the future, both the lenders and borrowers succumb to the short-term benefits and incentives of sub-par lending practices. Banks allowed less stringent verification of loan applicants, while borrowers become encouraged by the promise of flexible and more manageable interest rates. In the end, due to the disregard for the proven lending and borrowing system, the market crashed—causing the closure of several financial institutions and significant losses for the borrowers.

c. Mackenzie King, a former Canadian prime minister, discusses the similarities of Gresham's Law and the

Law of Competition, leading him to call the combined effects of both on the market as the "Law of Competing Standard".

According to him, the competing standards within the same industry become imbalanced when some companies chooses to do underhanded methods to lower their costs, thereby making their commodities or services more attractive to consumers. This can take various forms of unethical practices, such as illegally outsourcing labor into third-world countries, using sub-standard or even harmful materials, or padding products with unnecessary fillers.

Much like Gresham's observations about the disappearance of precious metals, the well-meaning intentions of companies to provide products and services that would be useful or helpful to the consumers would eventually become less of a priority to the industry. Instead, material gain would take precedence over quality and good customer service. Consumers might not realize at first the effect of this transition to the worse; Therefore, they would unwittingly strengthen the bad practices of the companies that offer cheaper commodities or services.

Prime Minister King then concluded that to prevent this from happening, high standards must be established as a basis for the checkpoints that will be applied by the industry to its players. Though it may be hard, he implored the different government agencies and private institutions to aid him in providing a guarantee of value for money to the consumers in general.

How Gresham's Law Can Improve Your Mental Models

Taking into account the phenomenon described by Gresham's Law, one could say that the best way to prevent the establishment of weak or destructive mental models is to put into place checkpoints on your own behavior. Employ a personal check-and-balance system to identify immediately bad practices and then recognize them for what they really are. They might benefit you in the short-term, but over time, continuing such bad practices could physically, emotionally, or mentally corrupt you.

In the event that the bad practice has already been ingrained in your system, the best way to handle such cases is to remove yourself from a permitting environment. Look for a more controlling environment that could keep you in line despite the urge to succumb to your impulses.

Without the chance to experience the supposed benefits of the bad practice, you would eventually realize that the negative effects of doing so overpowers whatever advantage you gain from it. Over time, the lack of opportunity to practice would also allow you to phase it out of your system and hopefully replace it with better and more ethical behaviors.

Mental Model in Systems: Pareto's Principle

Essentially, Pareto's Principle describes one of the so-called "universal truths" that 80% of the total output comes only from 20% of the input.

Historical Background

In the late 19th century, Italian philosopher and economist Vilfredo Federico Damaso Pareto first proposed his theory that 80% of the total results from only 20% of the actions done for a given activity. This idea stems initially while he was out in garden. As he was taking note of his harvest at that time, he realized that only about 20% of the pea plants produced almost 80% of the high-quality pea pods that he has harvested. This discovery led him to wonder if this imbalance of inputs and outputs also applies to other areas. To do this, he focused first on the obviously uneven wealth distribution in their country at the time. Upon examining the records of land ownership, he found out that only the 20% of the total population owned 80% of all the lands that can be owned by private citizens. Furthermore, he realized that only a vital few—the top 20% of the population—holds the power over the trivial many, or the bottom 80% of the country's population.

Searching for more proof, he turned his focus towards the different industries. He was pleased to learn that his theory continued to hold up. According to the data he has gathered, 80% of the total production for a given industry was generated by only 20% of the companies within that said industry. This observation remains consistent across various fields, so he concluded that his theory could be considered a generality.

Pareto's Principle in Action

Pareto's Principle is one of the most widely known concepts in business and economics. While the ratio is not always exactly 80:20, the logic behind this imbalance stands firm across different situations. For example:

- In the field of sales and marketing, only 20% of the total number of agents manage to generate 80% of the gross sales for a given period.

- A catering company observed that 80% of its profits come from only 20% of the clients they have handled.

- Software engineers of a particular word processing app noted that 20% of the reported software bugs have caused nearly 80% of the crashes of their software.

- The Department of Health reviewed its statistical data for a given year and discovered that 80% of the total spending on healthcare can be accounted to only 20% of the total population.

- Business executives have also noted the importance of applying the Pareto Principe in overcoming the challenges of having limited resources. Given the scope of their responsibilities, they do not only have manage their own time but also of their respective teams. Rather than aim for the impossible, the Pareto Principle allows them to figure out the priorities that would give them the most results. As for the rest of their probable goals, they could just put them aside for the time being, or even discard them completely.

- Many freelancers are using this principle sometimes without even realizing it. Since not all freelancers are fortunate enough to have a steady stream of work, they have to smart about choosing their clients. Aside from financial gains, it is also important for them to select only a few, but well-paying clients because having too many bosses at a given time can increase the likelihood of being burnt out.

- Given their nature, entrepreneurs are always tempted to go after and push through business ideas that may or may not pan out. To avoid wasting time and capital, some entrepreneurs apply this principle in order to determine whether or not a business is worth pursuing. After all, it is perfectly alright to take calculated risks, especially in business. However, this does not mean that they would have to witness all their efforts to go down the drain just because they do not know when to keep fighting and when to call it off.

How Pareto's Principle Can Improve Your Mental Models

The Pareto Principle can be applied to any situation, including your course to personal improvement. Learning which of your tasks and activities are essential to your success is a great way of putting direction and speed into this endeavor. Many experts also recommend the application of Pareto Principle into one's goal-setting exercises. Rather than simply making a list of the things you want to achieve, analyze the list further by identifying which of them should be your priority. By doing so, you are assured that you would get significant results, while still having some time left to do the other periphery goals in your list.

The Pareto Principle can also be of aid to those who have the tendency to procrastinate, especially at work. Many people tend to put off big tasks in favor of small doable tasks, thinking that these small steps would build and grow into something significant. However, studies show that doing the most complex tasks that comprise 20% of your list could give you tremendous rewards that you would not have gotten otherwise. Furthermore, if you develop a habit of doing only small, low-value tasks, you would eventually find it hard to complete the important, high-value activities that you should have prioritized in the first place.

Mental Model in Biology: Evolution by Natural Selection

Historical Background

The concept of evolution has long been introduced before Charles Darwin and his fateful voyage to Madagascar. What elevates the theory of Darwin is the evolutionary mechanism called natural selection. Through this, he was able to explain how certain organisms manage to adapt better with their respective environments compared to the others.

Darwin reached his concept of natural selection through the following key observations:

- Most traits can be passed by the parent organism to its offspring.

- Offspring are often produced beyond the number that can be reasonably sustained by their environment. As a result, competition arises over the limited resources available.

- Offspring that belong to the same generation vary from one another depending on the traits each has inherited from the parent. From these observations, Darwin arrived at the following conclusions:

  o Within a given population, certain organisms would inherit key traits that would make them more effective in terms of survival and reproduction compared to the other organisms of the same species who did not receive the same set of traits.

  o Because organisms with the helpful traits produce more

offspring, and because these helpful traits are heritable, there will be more organisms bearing these helpful traits, thus making the traits more common within their generation.

o   As time goes by, succeeding generations would be able to better adapt to the environment, making them more successful than their parents were at survival and reproduction.

The model of evolution that Darwin developed allowed him to make sense of the patterns that he had observed during his trip. For example, different species of a Galapagos finches share certain traits because they also share the same ancestors. However, if a certain group of organisms became isolated from the rest for several generations, that particular group develop a distinct set of traits that allowed them to survive and thrive in the environment of the island where they can be found. As a result, beaks of different shapes and sizes can be observed among the distinct species of finches that live in different islands of Madagascar.

Over the course of multiple studies conducted on Darwin's theory, experts on this mental model have managed to boil down its prerequisites into the following:

1. Replication - The ability to create new copies with a high level of fidelity with the immediate source

2. Mutation - The ability of the said copies to change in a slight, but potentially significant ways

3. Fitness - Copies should be able to persist and reproduce at various rates

When all three elements are present, you can expect the copies to survive and multiply with a high level of success. Copies that lack any of the given elements are likely going to die off, eventually.

Evolution by Natural Selection in Action

Over the years, Darwin's model of evolution by natural selection has gained popularity and massive support from the different communities. It should be noted, however, that not everything is capable of undergoing this process of evolution. To better understand this concept, there are some common answers of people when asked about the things that can evolve:

1. As evidenced by archaeological findings, homo sapiens has beat out other species, including Neanderthals and apes, among others. Believing that this is an evidence of evolution, however, is inaccurate. Following the three elements required for something

to evolve, replication is absent in this particular case. You might counter this by saying that humans replicate themselves by mating and producing children. Again, this is false because parents do not reproduce high-fidelity versions of themselves. The children will inherit certain traits from the mother and the father, but they will never be nearly exact copies of one or the other.

The correct answer, in this case, is that the human genes evolve. These are the building blocks of human evolution. Genes can replicate themselves over and over—with a small likelihood of undergoing mutation in the process.

2. Biological evolution is often the foremost example that comes to mind for most people. However, when analyzed carefully, cultural evolution also undergoes natural selection. First proposed by Joseph Henrich, the idea that human culture also evolves following similar patterns as genes do seem implausible. Upon closer examination, however, the three elements of evolution by natural selection are present whenever there is a shift in human culture.

In terms of replication, humans are natural at mimicking the behaviors of others, even without fully understanding the rationale behind the said action. By studying the ways of the people, they admire or respect, people are able to replicate with high fidelity certain aspects of other people's behaviors. Mutation plays a part because even though humans have high levels of skill when it comes to copying others, it is impossible to be perfect at all times. There are also instances where the initial copy is already wrong in some way, so when it gets replicated, the imperfection is passed on to more people.

The fitness of cultural behaviors is evident because humans only tend to mimic behaviors that they find beneficial or pleasing. Otherwise, the behavior will eventually die down until no one else would ever remember how to do it and why it was done in the first place.

Given these, one can argue that cultural practices are evolving by natural selection. A group's language, rituals, religions, and special tools are all part of the culture, and can therefore evolve as they get passed on to the younger generation.

How Evolution by Natural Selection Can Improve Your Mental Models There are various ways on how you can apply the principles of evolution by natural selection into your day-to-day life. First, you may be able to better assess the likelihood of success and longevity of the system you are creating by examining it against the core tenets of evolution by natural selection. Does your system provide opportunities for faithful replication? Is there an allowance for positive mutation? Does it exhibit signs of fitness? Answering yes to all of these questions is a good indicator that you are on the right track.

The concepts that define evolution by natural selection can also improve the way you solve problems. Rather than rely solely on logic, you may also come up with various approaches, mutate each one in slightly different ways, replicate, and then keep only the one that would work best.

Mental Model in Business: Scarcity

The reality of having limited resources and the possibility of having unlimited desires creates an economic phenomenon called scarcity.

Historical Background

Scarcity, as an economic force, has always been a looming presence in any community. There is, however, no exact record on who and when this was first formally defined. Many have attempted to dissect and study the causes and effects of scarcity, including renowned British economist Lionel Robbins. In one of his influential essays published in the early 20th century, Robbins elevated the concept of scarcity as one of the defining characteristics of the economy in general. He explained that without scarcity, there will be little or no driving force behind economic activities. Therefore, without scarcity, people would have lesser reason to compete with one another and strive for improvement and excellence.

Scarcity in Action

In the heart of scarcity lies the main question that almost everyone subconsciously asks to themselves: what is the most efficient and most effective way of using one's limited resources? Many have tried to provide a standard way of answering this, but scarcity can take many forms, and therefore requires different approaches, too.

To better understand this, examine the following examples of scarcity and its effects on everyone involved:

- People with training and experience in doing a particular skill are few and far in between. As such, the company employs the assistance of a recruitment agency to find these people, even if doing so adds up another 30% to the company expenses for recruitment and hiring.

- Contrary to what many people assume, water is not a renewable resource. Therefore, many environmental groups are campaigning for the proper and responsible usage of water, as well as for effective and efficient means of recycling used water for purposes other than drinking.

- The spectrum of frequencies is limited so telecommunication providers compete heavily amongst one another in order to get better and more allocation of frequencies for their services to the consumers.

- After a period of bad weather, the corn crops that the farmer planted earlier in the season failed to grow. This massive drop in harvest contributes to the food shortage experienced by both animals and people. A decrease in the production of ethanol fuel is also expected due to the lack of one of its main components.

- Due to the high costs of raising cows, there is a growing trend among farmers wherein former dairy farmers shift to other kinds of farming. As a result of the decreasing number of dairy products being produced, the market prices of dairy products, such as milk and cheese, increase.

- There are two possible outcomes for this price increase: consumers might continue to demand for dairy products, which would then attract dairy farmers back into raising cows, or consumers might be completely turned off by the inflation of prices, thereby prompting them to look for other viable alternatives to dairy products. In the case of the former, the price could go down and be stabilized once more, while the latter scenario would spell more doom for the dairy farming industry.

- The UN has imposed an embargo on imports to and exports from North Korea for the repeated offenses and non-compliances to human rights of the said country. Because of this, North Koreans would have a more difficult time accessing goods that are not being produced within their own land. Furthermore, the other countries that import goods from North Korea would experience shortages in the said goods until the embargo has been lifted. If the scarcity becomes even worse, the North Koreans might resort to buying and selling goods in the black market. However, doing so could create more problems that were not present before the embargo has taken effect.

- The spread of avian flu to Central America back in 2012 has caused the death of millions of birds, including chickens. This sudden death of the livestock caused a shortage of both eggs and chicken meat, both of which are staples in the typical Mexican kitchen.

How Scarcity Can Improve Your Mental Models

Recent studies on scarcity conclude that scarcity does not only affect one's economic decisions. It can also shape a person's decisions and behaviors. Therefore, scarcity is not simply felt physically. It also has significant effects on one's mind and emotions. In terms of improving your mental models, gaining a mindset that is centered around scarce resources would help you find out your true priorities. You would be able to identify which of your goals need to be achieved immediately and which ones can be ignored for the time being.

Scarcity could also essentially force you to be more creative when it comes to problem solving. Resolving issues caused by scarce resources is not as simple as one would think. To effectively survive and thrive without some of your basic needs, you need to be resourceful and clever, and then translate that into something sustainable for the entire duration of the scarcity.

Improving mental models can help you better understand life in general. It would give meaning and structure to your day-to-day activities and interactions with other people. Though they can be imperfect at times, you would always have the choice to change your course and mental models for the better.

Feel free to explore more examples of mental models and how others apply them into their respective lives and careers. The majority of the existing mental models come from broad areas of interest, other than business, economics, biology, and systems. Other interesting mental models are also derived from various concepts stemming from different fields, such as philosophy, chemistry, mathematics, and psychology.

Some experts argue that is essential for one to master at least one mental model from each field. By doing so, one would be able to get an exceptional grasp of how the world actually works. However, do not force yourself to do so right when you are just beginning to learn the principles behind mental models.

Let them come to you naturally as you go along your journey towards better thought processes. Welcome new concepts and keep an open mind while you examine them for their usefulness and applicability in your life. This is quite important because when it comes to mental modelling, the more diverse your set of schemas are, the richer your understanding of the world would be.

Chapter 5 – Start Connecting the Dots

The best mental models are the ones that you can apply in your day-to-day life. Each mental model has its own benefits and drawbacks. The key, therefore, is identifying the areas in your life where you can effectively use them.

By understanding these mental models vis-à-vis your thoughts and behaviors, you would be able to gain wisdom and improve yourself even further. Expand beyond what you already know and believe and consider that there might be better ways of doing things that matter to you.

The Role of Gresham's Law on Your Goal to Become a Better Person

The concept of the bad driving out the good does not only apply to the circulation of currency. In any aspect of your life, there would always be the possibility of the negative elements overpowering positivity until the latter is eventually phased out completely.

Gresham's Law highlights the dynamics that exist in this process, as well as the kind of environment that promotes such outcomes. To apply this into your life, you need to undertake the following steps. For each step, examine the three sample scenarios on how you could go about it yourself.

Step #1: Identify areas in your life that need to be improved. Reflect on why you think this change should be a priority for you.

a. Gary is a chain smoker since he had first learned how to smoke back in high school. Recently, he noticed that this bad habit has been taking its toll on him. Various throat and respiratory problems, such as sore throat, cough, and pneumonia, begin plaguing him one after the other. Though he does not know where to start, Gary believes that he needs to stop smoking soon before he contracts more serious forms of illnesses.

b. Jenny works as a HR manager for a startup company. Her role in the company is vital, especially since the turnover rate in the said company is higher than the industry standards. She needs to figure out why the employees are leaving so soon after she has just hired them. Otherwise, she might be out of the job soon as well.

c. Bryan, a closeted gay man, is feeling the growing pressure of toxic masculinity from some of his friends at the university. He does not want to come out to them in fear of losing his friends, but he also does not want to pretend that he is interested in women like them. Without anyone else to turn to, Bryan tries to smoke marijuana in order to escape from his reality. He knows that this is wrong, but he cannot think of any possible solution at the moment. What he knows right now is that this could easily turn into a dependence that would haunt him for the rest of his life.

Step #2: Check if your environment has any checkpoints or monitoring systems in place.

a. Gary lives in an apartment building that permits smoking only within the tenants' respective units. No one is allowed to smoke in the common areas, such as the hallways, lobby, or the laundry room. At work, a strict no-smoking policy has been recently implemented, in line with the new environmental and health law that has been passed in Congress. As long as the employee is within company premises, they are not allowed to consume any type of cigarette or other forms of smoking device. Many employees, including Gary, have complained about the inconveniences of this policy. However, with his recent realization about his personal health, Gary is now viewing this as some sort of divine providence.

b. Reviewing the exit interviews conducted with resigned employees, Jenny takes note of their comments and complaints about the company in general. She noticed that the majority of them are centered around office politics. While reflecting on this, Jenny realizes that one of the favorite pastimes of many employees here is to gossip amongst themselves. No one actually has made a formal complaint about this before, so she has never made any effort to discourage employees from doing so. Their employee manual does, however, prohibit non-productive activities, but it does not specify which types of activities fall under this. Another question that eludes her at the moment is the appropriate disciplinary action for this. How would she even objectively investigate cases that involve gossip within their office? Burdened by more questions than answers, Jenny decides to do more research on how to better handle this matter.

c. Bryan is not particularly assertive about his preferences and boundaries, so he usually just goes with the flow. No one in his group of friends are sensitive enough, however, to sense his discomfort whenever they go to parties, and try to pick up girls. When he started smoking marijuana, a couple of his friends begin spending more time with him. They bond over this shared activity, talking about whatever topic comes into their minds. Though their other friends do not mind Bryan's new habit, the university does have rules against illicit drugs and other substances. However, Bryan cannot recall if there has been any reported case regarding this, so he assumes that no one in the administration is actually assigned to implement these rules, and monitor the compliance of the students.

Step #3: Fully commit yourself to self-improvement.

According to Gresham's Law, you may proceed with either or both of the following options depending on what kind of environment you are in—as you have determined in step #2. If your environment has regulating measures, then you must commit to stop giving in to your negative or destructive tendencies, and to stick by the rules. On the other hand, if your environment lacks the said measures, consider first your other needs and wants in life before picking your next course of action. Based on your answer to this, you can either completely remove yourself from the dysfunctional environment that promotes whatever bad thoughts or behavior that you have, or you may put into place systems and checkpoints needed in order to mitigate the effects of your poor environment on you.

    a. Gary is indeed fortunate to live and work in environments that prohibit him from engaging in the behavior that he wants to stop doing. All he has to do is figure out how he could best go about it without sacrificing his happiness and quality of life. Gresham's Law does not have any provision on how Gary could go about this, so he would have to turn to other mental models in order to achieve his goal. This does not negate the effects that Gresham's Law had on Gary's road to self-improvement. Through this, he was able to realize that his bad habit is driving away the probability of him living a healthier and longer life. From there, he was also able to better appreciate the controls in his environment and understand the rationale behind such rules.

b. Jenny's environment lacks certain aspects that can still be corrected. She does not have to resign or be terminated from the company she works for because there are a lot of things that she could to change the dysfunctional working environment she has observed. For one, as the HR manager, she has the authority to request a review and revision of the employee manual. She would be able to better define the company policies and rules that would control and mitigate the effects of office politics on the work satisfaction of the employees.

Furthermore, Jenny and her team are also in charge of implementing these charges. She would have an active role in preventing the spread of bad elements in their system. Though it would definitely not be an easy task, it would be worth her while. She would be able to create a better working environment for the current staff, thereby potentially lowering the reported turnover rates in their company.

c. Bryan has a big decision to make. He can either remove himself entirely from the toxic environment he is in or be more open about his personal needs and boundaries with his friends. Removing himself from his current situation might seem like an unhealthy approach. However, as specified by Gresham's Law, you cannot hope to change the entire system when it is already outside your control, or if the environment itself cannot be regulated at all. Bryan cannot completely change the way his friends behave. He cannot forbid them to stop engaging in activities that make him uncomfortable.

Though it may sound extreme, Bryan could take a step away from his current group and seek other people who would understand his situation. On a lesser degree, he could also be more assertive about his limits and demand for his friends to respect his boundaries. Either way, there would be a distance between Bryan and his current dysfunctional environment. On the other hand, Bryan may also opt to be more open about his personal issues with his friends. He does not have to disclose his sexual orientation, but he may consider expressing his discomfort and asking for his friends' understanding. Bryan has no way of knowing completely how his friends would react to this, so he could take the chance and risk being more vulnerable in front of other people.

As you have read, Gresham's Law does not provide all the answers to the challenges imposed by negative schemas and weak mental models on a person. However, it does give answers to people who wish to eliminate bad elements in their system or remove themselves from unhealthy environments.

Applying the Pareto Principle in Different Aspects of Your Life

During the course of several studies, the Pareto Principle has consistently proven to everyone that it is one of the most helpful mental models for anyone looking for ways to improve their lives. Though it was first adapted by those in the fields of economics and business, the Pareto Principle can be applied in almost any aspect or interest. Before enumerating examples of good applications of this mental model, please note that the primary point of this principle is not the 80:20 ratio because not everything fits into this framing. Instead, the Pareto Principle highlights the imbalance between effort and output. Some things in life contribute more than others in the achievements of your goals. By adapting this kind of mindset, you would be able to set better goals and manage your resources.

To exhibit the versatility of the Pareto Principle, here are sample scenarios that you might have experienced yourself, and how each situation could benefit from the concepts of this mental model:

As one of Lucy's New Year resolution to embrace the minimalist lifestyle, she decided to start with her closet. Her dilemma began, however, when she had to choose which of her clothes should go and which should stay.

To handle this, she first sorted her clothes depending on how frequently she would them in a year. After a couple of hours, she found out that out of the ten cocktail dresses she owned, she only wore two of them for at least four different occasions in the past year. The rest were only worn once due to the various reasons. In order to make the most of her closet space, she decided to choose only the clothes that serve more than one purpose. She only kept dresses that could double as her work outfit and shirts that she could wear either to a party or to a casual dinner with her husband.

From having to occupy the entire closet just for her clothes, she was able to make space for extra beddings and pillows that they need whenever they have overnight guests. The rest of her unnecessary clothes would be donated to charity or sold to thrift shops where they could be better used by others. Given the free rein on how to spend his spring break, Nathan made a list of activities that he would want to do with his family and friends. His list ended up being too long for him to actually do everything in the list. The issue about the budget for these activities had also come to

him since he would have to pay for himself—
if not treat others as well.

To trim down the list, he rated each activity
depending on how long it would take, and
how enjoyable it would be for him and his
companions. He also researched on how
much each activity would probably cost him.
Having rated each item on his list, Nathan
ranked the average ratings and sorted the
activities from the highest rating down to the
lowest. After looking through his list once
more, he found out that the top 20% of his list
would fit within his budget while ensuring that
he would the maximum amount of fun during

the limited number of days of his break from the university.

Amy is rushing through a diorama that is due for submission the following day. Given the amount of time left before the deadline, she knows for a fact that not all sub-tasks would be finished on time. She needs to get a passing grade, however, so she has to identify which parts should be prioritized, and which would not have much effect on her final grade.

To do this, she took a quick pause and identified the points of a diorama that needs attention. From her examination, she figured that she could forego the detailing on the trees and focus instead on the painting the background blue to represent the sky. In her imagination, this would give a better impression that the diorama is actually finished.

Furthermore, the tree detailing—even though it would add value—takes up more time than simply painting a makeshift sky. Following this course of action, the end product appears similar to what she had in mind even though the level of detail is not as high as she was hoping it would be. The teacher also took similar notes of her project, but since it looks like a completed work, Amy was given the passing grade that she was expecting to get.

Scarcity and Its Effects on Your Decisions and Lifestyle

As explained in the earlier chapter, scarcity can become an integral part of one's mindset. Consider the aspects of your life that could be affected by having limited resources. What do you think would happen to you when you believe that you only have too little of what you need at the time? How would such a scenario affect your thoughts and actions?

According to experts, scarcity redefines the orientation of a person's mind. It causes everyone affected to focus on fulfilling unmet needs. For example, those who are starving have no choice but to seek ways to get food whenever and wherever possible. A lonely person, on the other hand, might go for any activity that would address their issues with social isolation and lack of personal connection with other people. If you have chosen to adapt this mental model, here are the possible ways that scarcity could change the way you think, decide, and act:

- Scarcity can improve your strategies on effectively and efficiently managing your goals.

    For example, the pressure of working within a deadline requires you to work with your full attention—or at least a majority of it—in order to finish the task on time, while still retaining the expected quality from you. The distractions from your environment, such as menial household chores or your favorite TV show, become less potent and thereby less tempting.

Another example is senior college students who only have a limited time left to enjoy being in the university and spending quality with their friends. As such, many go all out by hosting or attending parties and other social events. Some even create lists of things they must experience before formally entering the stage of adulthood.

- Scarcity allows you to break down your goals into small, doable tasks. Dealing with scarce resources requires you to be better at allocating your time and effort. For instance, you are working on a big project that can either make or break your career. The pressure of achieving your objectives can be too overwhelming for someone who wants to do everything all at once.

Scarcity forces you to concentrate on working through your priorities. The project would be broken down into smaller, but manageable chunks of work to do, all of which are aligned towards what would help you reach your goal for this project. By adapting the scarcity mental model, you would be able to make better use of your limited resources. Your chances of being paralyzed by the pressure or being burnt out in the process of attempting to have it all will be lessened significantly.

- Your experiences in life can be enriched by having a scarcity mindset. A renowned professor of philosophy once said that when people have the luxury of time, they feel no urgency to do anything worth their while. Essentially, living a life without limits makes everything appear dull and lacking.

Following this line of thinking, one could say that scarcity can be of help to those who are experiencing a mid-life crisis. At this point in one's life, the feelings of discontent and boredom increases exponentially, usually because the person has been doing the same things over and over again for the past few decades of his or her life. As a result, fatigue sets in, which then leads to a full-blown mid-life crisis when left unaddressed.

Scarcity can help people resolve their issues at this stage because it would force them to accept the inevitable reality of human mortality. The illusion that one can be anything and do everything would eventually dissipate once the person realizes that this is not possible anymore due to the limited time left.

As a result of this reorientation, the person would be able to build again confidence and restructure his or her priorities on what really matters. People would be able to overcome the issues that crop up during the period of their mid-life crisis once they accept the fact that there are many things in life that they cannot and should not do anymore.

- Scarcity provides you the opportunity to better assess the value of things. When you spend $5 on something, that also means you have $5 less on something else that you could have purchased instead. This opportunity cost, as the economists refer to it, causes you to pause and evaluate if you actually need something rather than the other thing that you are also considering getting. People with a scarcity mindset recognize the truth that having something means that you are not likely going to have the other thing too.

Having this kind of attitude makes you appreciate more the decision you have made, such as when you purchase a particular brand and model of a laptop among the other laptops offered in the same shop. Thinking that you would be able to get two or three of your options would be a waste of resources that you could have spent on other essential things. Therefore, you choose the one that fits best your requirements, and in the process, learn how to be content with the decisions that you make in life.

Making the Most Out of Your Mental Models

People who are just beginning to consciously adapt mental models are prone in making the mistake of sticking only to one or two models that seem to fit their needs the best. This overdependence causes them to use their favorite mental model to make sense of the world they live in. As time goes on, the familiarity of a few chosen mental models would lull them into thinking that they could always depend on these models no matter what the situation is.

The problem with this kind of mindset is that when a particular mental model dominates your way of thinking, you would fall into the habit of trying to explain everything through that perspective. Even when facts contrary to this has been presented, you would not easily accept the truth of the matter.

A classic example of a scenario exhibiting this is first presented by Robert Sapolsky, a biologist and believer of using different mental models to improve the quality of one's thinking and decision-making skills. He cited the following responses of different experts on the question, "Why did the chicken cross the road?"

- A neurologist responded by explaining how the neurons in the chicken's brain were triggered thus prompting the said behavior of the chicken.

- An expert on body movements said that the muscle in the chicken's thighs, legs, and feet contracted and pulled the bone in each limb.

- An evolutionary biologist, on the hand, replied by assuming that the chicken probably saw a potential mate from across the street.

When viewed from the perspective of their given fields, none of these answers are technically wrong. However, no one is exactly seeing the whole picture, thus the varied responses that a single question got from these individuals. The same principle applies to mental models and one's perspective about reality. Focusing and applying only on one or two mental models for every aspect in your life would turn you into a narrow-minded and obstinate individual.

To further expound on this, here is an example of a common real-life scenario wherein you can combine multiple mental models in order to improve your approach in clearing obstacles in your way and reaching your goals in the best way possible.

Sandra wants to lose the extra twenty pounds she has gained over the past few months. To prepare for this, she researches the various weight loss methods as recommended by dieticians and lifestyle gurus. The mountain of information she has amassed, however, is making her feel overwhelmed about how and where to start. Furthermore, since summer is only three months away, she has given herself only three months at most to accomplish her desired weight.

One of Sandra's friend pushes her to make an analysis of her current situation and goals through the perspective of the following mental models: Gresham's Law, the Pareto Principle, and the scarcity mindset. Together, these three mental models could give a solid foundation and structure to her personal weight loss program, as well as facilitate her progress towards her fitness goals.

Mental Model #1: Gresham's Law

The best way to start Sandra's journey towards significant weight loss is to analyze if her current environment would support her initiatives and attempts to change her lifestyle. Here are her key observations that led her to vital realizations that have significant impacts on how she could design an effective weight loss program for herself:

- Sandra buys takeout food whenever she has to eat alone because she does not want to cook for just a single person.

- During dull times at work, Sandra finds herself reaching for a box of sweets on her desk. She decides to keep count of how many pieces she would consume, and she discovers that she could easily eat 5 pieces of toffee candy in one afternoon.

- Whenever she feels upset or depressed, Sandra indulges herself by buying or cooking her favorite comfort food: a bowl of mac and cheese. Depending on how intense her feelings are, she would either make this from scratch or just cook it straight from the box.

- Sandra has always led a primarily sedentary lifestyle, except for moments where her friends would invite her to join them in the local gym. She does acknowledge the merits of exercising regularly, but her motivational levels fluctuate depending on the mood of her friends.

- Sandra prefers drinking sugared drinks, such as soda and fruit juices, after a meal. She only drinks water whenever her preferred drinks are not available to her at that given moment. Distilling the important points from her observations, Sandra concludes that in order to increase her chances of success, she needs to:

- o Lessen the amount of takeout food that she consumes. According to her research, takeout food has significantly higher levels of fats, calories, and salt compared to home-cooked meals. To do this, she either has to make time for cooking meals for herself or invite her friends and family over to cook and eat together.

- Remove the fattening foods away from her reach. Sandra has to store her box of candies and other snacks in a place that is far enough to dissuade her from taking the time to get it. She also needs to find other ways to relieve herself from boredom or intense feelings, such as getting up from her seat and taking a quick walk outside or practicing meditation techniques.

- Request for the cooperation of her friends. In order to lose weight, Sandra has to get up from a seat, and exercise regularly. Since she rarely, if ever, initiates this, her friends could step in, and provide her the much-needed boost she needs to fulfill this part of her personal weight loss program.

o Phase out sugared drinks from her daily diet. Going cold turkey is never the right answer. Instead, Sandra could gradually replace her usual beverages with a glass of water until she could get used to this. She should also avoid including this in her grocery list, so that she would not have any other choice but to drink water whenever she eats at home.

Reviewing these given points, you could surmise that Sandra has high control over her environment. This means that with the right strategy she would be able to turn around her situation and remove the unwanted elements in her system—the excess body weight, that is.

Mental Model #2: Pareto Principle

Sandra is fortunate to have various routes that she could take on her quest to weight loss. However, she needs to be smart about choosing which one to follow, especially she has only a limited amount of time to accomplish her desired weight. In order to better assess her strategies to lose weight, her friend helps her evaluate her options with the use of the Pareto Principle. To save time, they decide to use the following guide questions:

- Which food items or beverages contribute the most to Sandra's weight gain?

- What exercise routine can Sandra adapt in order to quickly lose weight without having to expend so much time and energy at the gym?

Looking back at her earlier personal assessments, Sandra decides to cut back on her consumption of sweets and sugared beverages. She believes these items are detrimental to her goals and contribute nothing much on keeping her fit and healthy while she strives to lose the extra pounds. In terms of exercise, Sandra and her friends makes a list of exercise routines that they could do together, and then rank them according to the amount of time and effort needed to do them regularly. From this, they are able to determine that the optimal exercise routine for them is jogging around the park every morning.

Neither of these initiatives completely guarantee Sandra's success in shedding off 20 pounds from her total weight. However, compared to her other options, these two offer the most rewards and benefits while only requiring minimal effort on her part. Because of this, Sandra would have an easier time in committing to her strategies rather than trying to do a total overhaul of her diet and fitness routines.

Mental Model #3: Scarcity

Recognizing time as a limited resource would help Sandra maintain her focus on what matters the most in terms of her goal to lose weight. By doing so, she would be able to better resist temptations that would lead her astray from her goals. For example, during her monthly period, Sandra suddenly gets a craving for her favorite cookies. Rather than head down the local bakery, she tries to come up with other healthier options that would not contribute much on her daily calorie intake. Adapt a mindset centered around scarcity also enables her to appreciate more every single sacrifice that she has to make in order to achieve her goals. As a result, the likelihood of losing sight of what she aspires to become would be decreased significantly. Guided by these mental models, Sandra is now better equipped at handling the challenges that may come in her way as she continues to pursue her goals. It is important to remember, however, that she is not restricted to following the same mental models throughout her course. Depending on what needs to be done, she could adapt new models or drop some, as long as she does not waver from what she ultimately wants to achieve.

Expanding your set of mental models is not only something you should aspire for, but something you need in order to continually improve yourself. Furthermore, you should not be content with the current state of your mental models. Everyone has the option to increase the quality of how they view and understand the world in general. Mental models are not set in stone. They evolve over enough time and gain more knowledge from different sources. When this happens to your mental models, you would be able to not only pursue your initiatives for personal improvement, but it would also strengthen the relationships you have with the people you care about.

Chapter 6–Keep Track of Your Progress

Adapting a mental model takes time and effort. It is not something that you can do successful in one day or even a whole week's time. As such, it is important to keep track of how well you are doing in order to appreciate how far you have gone in terms of improving your set of mental models.

As a popular saying goes, "It takes 21 days to form a new habit." Though many have tried to refute this, the grain of truth behind these remains consistent despite the various suggestions on the exact number of days.

Creating a habit out of your mental models is an excellent way to assure that you would be following their guidance, even if you get the impulse to revert back to your old ways of thinking. Therefore, to aid you in this step of the process, here is a simple table that you can use to monitor your daily compliance with your chosen mental models.

<u>Table 1 Suggested Progress Tracker</u>

Mental Models	Sunday	Monday	Tuesday	Wednesday	Thursday	Friday	Saturday
1							
2							
3							
4							

Learning how to use this table would only take you a couple of minutes. If you still have the list you have made from the first chapter, use that as a point of reference about the things that you could improve upon in your life.

Follow these instructions to get a better grasp on this table could help you. To illustrate each step, imagine being in Sandra's shoes while she strives to lose 20 pounds off her weight—as described in the previous chapter.

1. Fill out the first column with your preferred mental models.

For example:

Mental Models	Sunday	Monday
Gresham's Law		
Pareto Principle		
Scarcity		

2. Each day, write down on the respective empty cells the instances where you have followed a particular mental model. Do not force yourself by make contrived entries. Be honest about your day-to-day experiences so that you would be able to better determine your progress later on.

For example:

Mental Models	Sunday	Monday
Gresham's Law	I declined an invitation from my parents to dine out at the local fast food restaurant. Instead, I asked them if they want t come over at my place so we could cook and eat together as a family.	
Pareto Principle		I jogged twice around the park across the street with my best friend, Maisie. She's the best!
Scarcity		Passed by a food truck on our way to the apartment. I was tempted for a quick second, but I decided against it when I remembered that I still have some leftovers from last night's dinner with my family.

3. By the end of the week, make a tally of the number of instances you have described for each mental model.

For example:

Mental Models	Week 1
Gresham's Law	4
Pareto Principle	7
Scarcity	5

4. Reflect on the summary you have gotten for the given week. How many days have you successfully followed your chosen mental models? What factors caused you to stray from your mental models? Do you think that

your set of mental models are at their optimal levels? Or is it time to re-evaluate them again, and see where if you could do better?

For example:

Sandra wrote in her reflection journal, "I am so happy about learning how to follow the 80-20 rule. Now, I know that I don't have to spend a whole lot of time and effort to get significant results."

5. Repeat steps 1 through 4 until you have accomplished a whole month's worth of monitoring. By the end of the month, assess once more the effectiveness, efficiency, and appropriateness of your chosen mental models vis-à-vis your current needs and

wants. You can also put these in terms of percentage to get a more objective sense of how well you have done.

For example:

Mental Models	Week 1	Week 2	Week 3	Week 4	Total	Percentage
Gresham's Law	4	5	4	6	19	67%
Pareto Principle	7	6	6	7	26	92%
Scarcity	5	6	7	6	24	85%

Remember, the main goal of this exercise is to keep you highlight the importance of regular practice in improving your mental models and eliminating weak and negative ones from your system. Without knowing how you are doing, you might get lost in the process, and forget why you have even chosen a particular mental model in the first place.

Applying Mental Models in Your Daily Life

Learning about mental models from books like this one is just the start of your journey towards better thoughts, attitudes, decisions, and actions. In order to gain complete mastery over your chosen mental models, you need to learn how to apply them in your day to day life. By doing so, you are going to gain familiarity on how to use them properly, when the right time is to use them, and how to continually improve them.

To do this, all you need is to follow these tips:

1. Read

   Your knowledge about your current
   mental models, and other models that
   could be of help to you, diversifies as
   you read about the thoughts of other
   people. As you go through their
   arguments and opinions, you may find
   yourself agreeing or refuting the points
   that they are making. That, by itself, is a
   good sign that your mental models are
   thriving, and that you remain open-
   minded to possible points of
   improvement in your current thought
   processes.

2. Store

Merely consuming information would not get you the results you are expecting for. You need to be able to retain important parts of it so that you can look back at that whenever you need a refresher. Keeping a personal journal is helpful especially when you are aiming for self-improvement. Nowadays, you have the option of doing it through traditional means or switching to digital note-taking apps. Feel free to do whatever works best for you.

3. Connect

You cannot fully master a particular mental model when you cannot see how it correlates with other mental models. You need to learn how to see how one affects the others when viewed from a realistic perspective. Comparing and contrasting different mental models is one of the effective approaches to achieve this level of understanding. Many find this easier to achieve by writing down their thoughts in their personal journals.

4. Trigger

Once you have gained a high level of understanding of a particular mental model, you would be able to recognize the signs of where and when to use them. Triggers are helpful because they prompt you to use your mental models in thinking or behaving in a more effective and efficient manner. Without these triggers, you would only have a notebook full of notes about mental models and what you should be doing with them.

Developing your personal set of mental models takes dedicated practice and commitment from you. Acquiring them could happen one at a time, so be patient in figuring out which models would actually fit best with your needs and wants in life.

Conclusion

I'd like to thank you and congratulate you for transiting my lines from start to finish. I hope this book was able to help you to discover how mental models improve your quality of thoughts, decisions, and actions.

The next step is to reflect upon your current status in life and assess how well your mental models fit with your lifestyle. Also, it is important to examine if your mental models are serving the correct purpose. If you believe that they are bordering upon being a stereotype, a prejudice, or a form of cognitive bias, then take some time to evaluate further this aspect of your mental processes. Only when you are aware of your areas for improvement, could you hope for something in your life to change for the better. As explained in the earlier chapters, mental models work best when used in an effective combination. Think of them as the eyes of your mental processes. Each mental model is capable of seeing different perspectives—some have similar ranges of vision, while others are capable of viewing the blind spots of other mental models. This means that utilizing them whenever necessary increases your chances of being successful in thinking, deciding, and acting in more effective terms.

Unfortunately, if you cover one of these eyes, you would not be able to get the complete picture of things. You are likely going to miss out important details that should have been obvious to you, if only you have kept that side of you open to the truths of the world.

If you are hesitating from choosing a set of mental models to follow, do not fret because that is a natural reaction among beginners. Remember, there is no correct formula that works for everybody.

In addition, you do not have to be a master of all the available mental models out there. Of the thousands of mental models from different fields of interest, you only need to get a good grasp of some of them so that you could gain a multi-disciplinary perspective of

how the world works.

Author's Note

If there was one thing that you learned from reading this book, what would it be? All you need is that one key learning to take you to the next steps in your journey to becoming more self-aware of your personal strengths and weaknesses.

The only way to keep this learning alive is by sharing it with a friend or a colleague who can benefit from it. In doing so, you are creating a network of people who can keep the conversation alive around the topic that you've just read.

In the end of all this, I hope that you have found your golden nugget/s throughout reading this book. Your success is my success.